NEW MOTHERHOOD

NEW MOTHERHOOD
Cultural and Personal Transitions in the 1980s

MIRA CROUCH

School of Sociology
The University of New South Wales
Sydney, Australia

and

LENORE MANDERSON

Tropical Health Program
The University of Queensland Medical School
Brisbane, Australia

Gordon and Breach Science Publishers

Switzerland • Australia • Belgium • France • Germany • Great Britain
India • Japan • Malaysia • Netherlands • Russia • Singapore • USA

Gordon and Breach Science Publishers

Y-Parc
Chemin de la Sallaz
CH-1400 Yverdon, Switzerland

Post Office Box 90
Reading, Berkshire RG1 8JL
Great Britain

Private Bag 8
Camberwell, Victoria 3124
Australia

3-14-9, Okubo
Shinjuku-ku, Tokyo 169
Japan

58, rue Lhomond
75005 Paris
France

Emmaplein 5
1075 AW Amsterdam
Netherlands

Glinkastrasse 13–15
O-1086 Berlin
Germany

820 Town Center Drive
Langhorne, Pennsylvania 19047
United States of America

Library of Congress Cataloging-in-Publication Data

Crouch, Mira, 1932–
    New motherhood : culural and personal transitions in the 1980s /
Mira Crouch and Lenore Manderson.
        p.   cm.
    Includes bibliographical references and index.
    ISBN 2-88124-945-0
    1. Mothers--Australia--Attitudes.   2. Motherhood--Australia.
3. Childbirth--Australia.   4. Australia--Social conditions.
I. Manderson, Lenore.   II. Title.
HQ759.C93 1993
306.874'3'0994--dc20
                                                                93-14102
                                                                CIP

CONTENTS

PART THREE
BEFORE AND AFTER THE EVENT

PART FOUR
AFTERTHOUGHTS

ACKNOWLEDGMENTS

Lists define and limit; they exclude as they include. Naming those who contributed to this book would fail to reflect the many ways in which family, friends and colleagues have, over the years, contributed to our knowledge and understanding, both of our work and the society in which we live. There are, even so, a few specific contributions that we wish to acknowledge. Funding was provided to support initial fieldwork from the Special Research Grant Scheme of the Faculty of Arts, The University of New South Wales, and additionally by the Tropical Health Program of the Faculty of Medicine, The University of Queensland. Carla Hankins and Leanne Thompson conducted some of the interviews in Sydney and Gosford, and Andrea Whittaker later assisted in analysis; we are very grateful to them for their contributions. We are grateful also to Rena Wright for her invaluable assistance in the final preparation of the manuscript.

In particular, we wish to thank the women who were involved in this project, who shared their experiences and ideas with us. Their interest in and enthusiasm for the project provided us with the impetus to see it through.

PART ONE
INITIAL CONCEPTIONS

Introduction

OUR AGENDA, AMONG OTHERS

This book is concerned with women's transition to parenthood—with conception, pregnancy, labour and delivery, and the first few months of mothering. In it we have sought to identify major themes of women's experiences of these events and, in turn, interpret them in the light of prevailing cultural concerns and social circumstances. Our research was undertaken between 1982 and 1987, comprising multiple interviews with 93 women, each of whom gave birth to her first child during this period. In addition to the interviews, we also carried out participant observation of labour, childbirth education classes and mothers' meetings. We have chosen to reflect on this material over an extended period of time, allowing a degree of wisdom of hindsight to enhance, we feel, our understanding of a decade marked by intense interest in the social and cultural practices of reproduction.

This interest in reproduction during the 1980s has been displayed in both public and academic reportage and debate covering a wide range of issues: the technology of reproduction, women's rights over the management of pregnancy and birth, critiques of obstetrics and women's health care, and definitions of femaleness that have constellated around an understanding of the importance of women's ability to reproduce. Inevitably, some of the contemplation of our research material incorporates our responses to its intellectual context.

The growth of interest through the 1980s in reproduction stands in marked contrast to the 1970s, a decade characterised—most particularly through the energy and writings of the women's movement—by a critical stance towards reproduction in so far as the processes of reproduction were seen to provide the basis for the structural subordination of women and their domination by men. Freedom, equality and personal autonomy were often represented as goals antithetical to childbearing and rearing; as a consequence numbers of women chose not to have children, *at least for a while*. That the decision to defer or reject childbearing was a minority movement—confined, possibly, to middle-class women with careers and "self-actualisation" in mind—is reflected by birth statistics during the period (Australian Bureau of Statistics, 1990; for the US and UK respectively, see Toliver, 1986 and Kiernan, 1988). Nevertheless, the critiques of motherhood and mothering were picked up in the popular media, and women who already had children felt keenly their liminality within the women's movement.

As a result of this perception of reproduction as an institution that controlled and oppressed women, the political energy of the 1970s concentrated, at least to some extent, on resistance to maternity through the advocation of women's rights both to equity in public life and to abortion and safe family planning to ensure that pregnancy was a genuine option. By the end of the 1970s, however, there had been some negotiation of this stand, a shift with a new interest in the feminine (however defined) and in the ways of power, influence and control that were unique to women. A number of feminists had begun to reassess their own political agenda and, in rejecting male values and structures, to appreciate activities, experiences and roles that were exclusively if not universally female (Ruddick 1980, 1989). Childbearing was one obvious activity.

A re-embracing of pregnancy and birth, and of the ability and desirability to reproduce—given the continuing disadvantages to women in terms of their mobility, opportunities and status as a result of childbearing—created obvious tensions. Although writers criticising *in vitro* fertilisation and related reproductive technologies continued to argue against the "essentialist" presumptions which sustained perceptions of a demand for such technologies, the decade was more popularly one of general approbation of motherhood, at least as *part* of women's experience. What was contested was (simply) the mode of mothering (for example the degree to which women might combine motherhood and paid employment) and conservative understandings that continued to characterise women firstly or primarily as mothers.

The political re-instatement of motherhood (by feminist writers) coincided with the tangibly increased participation of women in the workforce, their improved economic status (in general) and a greater liberalism and tolerance towards alternative domestic arrangements. The weakening emphasis on the conventional family was much pushed by the rising divorce rate and increases in single-parent and "blended" families. While most women through the 1980s (and today) in fact have borne children within stable heterosexual unions, there has been an increase in single motherhood; indeed single motherhood has become an acceptable part of the global embrace of "mother" as a value. There has been, in addition, a rise in the average age of first births, reflecting a blowing out of the age at which a woman may be regarded, in lay terms, as elderly *primigravida*—the lifting of the ceiling for reproduction and a decline in the notion of a "biological clock" that begins to tick at the age of 30.

The 1980s thus saw an increased acceptance of single mothers (although one should note, not adolescent single mothers), older mothers, and lesbian mothers. This was consistent with the re-evaluation of motherhood: a sloughing-off of the most intransigent vestiges of traditional attitudes and of the prescriptions that have governed reproduction (in terms of time, social relationships and context), but without challenging the ideas that have coloured women's own sense of self as informed by their maternity. In this lies the explanation, in part, of the symbolic weight of infertility and the demand for access to reproductive technology, notwithstanding its critics.

Parallel to this embrace of reproduction and, at the same time, wider access to contraception, was a decline in the number of single women who gave birth and surrendered their infants for adoption. In the space of some twenty years, adoption as an option for Australian women all but died out. In the 1950s, for example, working class girls adopted out-of-wedlock infants to middle class couples, thereby meeting the needs then—before technology provided an alternative—of those couples to reproduce (Harper, 1992)[1]. At the time when adoption was common, the right was upheld both of a couple to have children and for the couple and adopted child to be "matched" through adoption registration processes that monitored, as far as possible, ethnic background, phenotype and sometimes, social background. But by the 1970s, adoption had ceased to be a significant option for Australians wishing to parent. At the same time, as we shall discuss further below, attention shifted to the individual's experience of having a child, rather than creating a family. Hence the lure of reproductive technology, the role of science in overcoming the recalcitrance of biology to realise both personal desires and social goals.

It would seem that by the 1980s, there had been a crystallisation of trends into an interest in the mother/child unit, ideologically as well as practically. For example, state support through social welfare benefits was provided to enable single mothers to stay home rather than to work. Yet at the same time, there was apparent also a growing expectation that motherhood and paid work were activities to be combined—hence the popular image of the "supermum". The revision of attitudes to reproduction continued to reflect middle class values: the typical image of the 1980s was of a woman who had both a career and children (one or two); she was never, of course, a woman with three children, a housing commission flat, and a *casual* job as a check-out "girl" at the local Safeways.

While the media continued to manipulate the images of achievement to allow childbearing as part of—indeed an essential component of—the successful woman, they also focused on the actual events of pregnancy and birth. Here, the interest in the *doing* of pregnancy and birth was one that aligned some feminists with a range of other groups: the Nursing Mothers' Association,

---

1. cf. Spensky (1992) for the UK.

homebirth activists, critics of hospital-based medicine, and most recently advocates of the "New Age". As motherhood became increasingly a commodity and object for consumption, the development of support networks and voluntary special interest associations paralleled the growth of professional interests in birth and motherhood.

The phenomenology of pregnancy and birth remained largely outside of the scope of these interests, except for anthropologists concerned with childbirth in cultures other than their own. It was in response to this that Ann Oakley published, in edited form, the transcripts of interviews held with British women, as a means of making accessible "at home" women's perceptions and experiences of childbirth and childrearing. This she regarded as a prelude to and a precondition for the sociological analysis of maternity. *Becoming a Mother* was published first in 1979; the Penguin edition—retitled *From Here to Maternity* and published in 1981 and, with a new introduction, again in 1986—is a testimony to its popularity, to the skill with which Oakley presents women's histories of childbirth, and to its pioneer status in the sociology of reproduction.

The book is compelling reading: over 545 hours of recorded interviews edited to highlight the variety of women's experiences in becoming mothers. The experiences presented in this book— women's reactions to and accommodation of pregnancy, anticipation of parenting, the experiences of labour and delivery, and adjustment to the new infant and the early months of motherhood—are used as linchpins of a developing sociological model of maternity, one that is elaborated and refined in Oakley's later volume, *Women Confined* (1980).

From Here to Maternity served as a catalyst for subsequent research but also reflected contemporary thinking in the area. It appeared at a time when other theorists were drawing attention to the particular vulnerability of women to specialist obstetricians and gynaecologists, and when feminists had begun to question the lack of control by women over the processes of reproduction and to document the decline of midwifery as an autonomous and woman-centred/woman-directed profession. It echoed certain like works, such as Suzanne Arms' angry criticism of obstetric practice in the United States (1975); or Sheila Kitzinger's survey of cross-cultural birth practices (1978) that probably found for her a new, wider audience of feminists and social scientists beyond her established following of midwives and home birth activists. In Australia, a number of related works appeared at around the same time,[2] reflecting a renewed interest in childbearing within the community at large. Among these, two biographical collections, Berwyn Lewis' *No Children by Choice* (1986) and Gloria Frydman's *Mature-Age Mothers* (1987) projected most tellingly through their dialogue the complex meanings of motherhood in the '80s.

Berwyn Lewis' book *No Children by Choice* (1986) comprises thirteen biographical accounts of decisions not to bear children, decisions that followed mostly from individual understandings of the association between parenting and loss of autonomy. Not all the contributors were in fact childless by choice by the time they spoke to Lewis and not all saw their childlessness as a necessarily desirable or permanent state. But the reasons offered for childlessness, where the decision was more clearly self rather than circumstantially determined, are instructive: it is noticeable, for instance, that contributors frequently alluded to the notion of their own childishness, and the need to be "fully adult" before taking on the responsibility of a child.

Other attitudes to motherhood provide perhaps a more expected background to the decision to remain childless. These include the negative image of motherhood as an identity and occupation; of motherhood as a symbol of mindlessness and of concomitant loss of liberty, isolation and loss of self—in contrast,

---

2. These include the early work of Lyn Richards and Jan Harper (Harper and Richards, 1979; Harper, 1980; Richards, L., 1985) and a subsequent wide range of books concerned with options of birthing, parenting, childcare, and childrearing; the meanings of mothering and the ideology of motherhood (Wearing, 1984); surrogacy and technological interventions (Crowe, 1985; Scutt, 1988; Rowland, 1990); autobiographical accounts of pregnancy, labour and delivery (Parents' Book Collective, 1986) and surrogacy (Kirkman and Kirkman, 1988), and the tensions as well as the joys of parenting (Nicholson, 1983).

for example, to a contributor of Frydman's book *Mature Age Mothers* (1987), who says that although having a baby is a major change, "you still feel you are you" (Frydman, 1987:139–140). But women's fear of being subsumed by the infant is real, echoed also by participants in more recent studies (see, for example, Myra in Kaplan, M.M. 1992:54–62). For some women (and men), the price is too great to pay. Others—like the contributors of Frydman's book—are prepared to pay this price: in their minds, to surrender liberty is the price of fulfilment. Whether either eventuates—loss of liberty, or the gain of fulfilment—is of course a separate question. What is of interest here is the way in which women juxtapose such extreme eventualities in their decision-making related to reproduction. The availability and reliability of contraception, and the widening of options for women as workers, as well as the increase in public reflection on the intrinsic values of mothering, have resulted in such self-conscious questioning.

Frydman's book, *Mature-Age Mothers* (1987), is structurally similar to Lewis'. It includes 18 case histories, mainly of Melbourne women; several are easily identifiable and well known to Australian readers. The women are all self-described "late mothers", although the definition of late motherhood is loose: the women are aged 30–42, and not all are first-time mothers; some had had other children in their late teens/early twenties.

The reasons for their delayed first or later pregnancies vary, although they are the same kinds of reasons that Lewis' contributors offer for not having children at all: career, lack of confidence, inability to make the necessary commitment, lack of a partner, the infertility of a partner, earlier disinterest in childbearing and children, their partner's resistance to parenthood. Each chapter is a biographical account of pregnancy, birth and early mothering, derived from an edited transcript of an interview (between each woman and Gloria Frydman). (Notably, most contributions contain detailed and, in some cases, quite lengthy accounts of labour and the circumstances and quality of the birth experience). The themes of these interviews include the association of "adulthood" and "womanhood" with reproduction: a fully adult woman, in this society as in most others, is a woman who has conceived, born and brought up a child. Women's own sense of personal development as well as their social status is related to child-bearing—which for many women also affirms the primacy and permanency of a relationship with another adult (usually the child's father). "Commitment", a concept nicely elaborated by Quinn (1982), is neither abstract nor conceptual here; it has an experiential dimension, in the form of shared pregnancy and birth, and a material dimension—the resultant child.

This literature on "having children" shows that women perceive a strong relationship between personal identity and childbearing. In subsequent chapters, we shall explore further the nature of this relationship, which, in the contemporary social context, is specific to each woman and thus needs to be individually carved out against a background of conceptions of womanhood which are linked with maternity in both normative and substantive terms.

Summarily, then, in the 1980s there surfaced a renewed sense of the importance of motherhood to women, theoretically and politically as well as personally. Motherhood is now seen not so much as the basis of women's social position (previously so funda-mental a perception), but rather as a significant component of their feminine being. The interest in childbirth, initiated during the 1970s by the feminist critique of medical interventions in labour, now signals a desire to secure not only the autonomy and control sought earlier, but also a particular quality of an experi-ence that represents an existential moment in women's lives. This shift took place during the last decade, at a time when many women had already developed an awareness and acceptance of their right to personal space and time and to self-expression and fulfilment in many spheres of life. Such expectations interacted significantly with the subjective experience of childbearing and women's concerns with it. So far, feminist research in this area has actively fostered, rather than examined, these concerns. At the end of a decade of change, we are able to articulate and analyse them in their social and cultural context which can now be viewed, to some epistemological advantage, with a backward glance.

Chapter 1

METHODS, LIMITS AND LIMITATIONS

Our study draws on the experiences, perceptions and under-standing of 93 women living, at the time of our work with them, in Sydney, Canberra and the Central Coast of New South Wales. We interviewed most of these women several times: at least once and often twice during pregnancy, and then up to four times within around the first six months post-partum. During these interviews women spoke to us of their expectations of mother-hood, their experiences of giving birth, the shaping of their lives with a newborn and their feelings concerning all these matters. We also discussed their perceptions of the place of motherhood in women's lives in the context of contemporary society as under-stood by them. From these personal narratives we have pieced together a pattern of themes and dimensions identifiable in new mothers' consciousness and have attempted, in turn, to locate this pattern in a matrix of significant factors in the cultural and social context of our time. This interview material has been read against the popular and academic literature of the period, including the extensive treatment given to motherhood—in many different ways—within the popular press; it was supplemented too by letters written to us by women who had learnt of the study, and by diaries kept by some of the women participating in the study.[3]

The rapid social changes of the last two decades have produced diverse and complex interactions of social structure, action and meaning, intricately interwoven and significant in detail. Therefore our methodology was chosen to be responsive to nuances of feeling and opinion as well as sensitive to subtleness and minutiae of situation and circumstance. We were also conscious of the need, in this study, to penetrate the elusive nature of emotional response and the comparative reticence of profound experience. The combined methods of focused interviewing (Merton *et al.*, 1956) and "analytic induction" (Znaniecki, 1934; Jones, 1979), employed within an ethnographic approach, allowed maximum flexibility in both the collection and interpretation of data, while enabling us to retain order by focusing on the development of concepts throughout the study. Such procedures were entirely consistent with our aim which was rather more to determine "what things 'exist' than to determine how many such things there are" (Walker, 1985:3). In this research, the fact that we are both women and mothers has been in many ways our most valuable methodological resource.

SAMPLING AND DATA-COLLECTION

For practical reasons, our sampling was accidental. Most, but not all, of the women we interviewed were middle-class, native

---

3. Social research on mothering and motherhood, undertaken over the past 10–15 years, has drawn on a range of methods to explain the cultural and personal meanings of motherhood, although many researchers have relied especially on in-depth interviews with varying sample sizes: as few as six women in Vangie Bergum's book *Woman to Mother* (1989); twelve middle class New York women in M.M.Kaplan's study (1991) which uses content analysis of two interviews per woman and a number of psychology tests to explore women's interpretations and enactment of motherhood; and various studies based on much larger samples. Our study, drawing on several interviews with each of 93 women and supplemented by participant observation, is among the largest of these.

Australian and white. Since the "results" of our study consisted of concepts and propositions concerning dimensions of experience and their social meanings (as against a corpus of descriptors), the comparative social homogeneity of our group of women aided, rather than hindered, our analysis. On a practical, processual level it facilitated communication with our informants. More importantly, however, on the theoretical plane it helped us to make inferences regarding the links between our findings and their cultural setting, since this setting is lodged, as well as represented, in the common-sense knowledge which is both influenced and publicly articulated by "players" from the middle class (Touraine, 1984). For this reason we hold that our interpretations may be generalised to prevailing circumstances and concerns in the particular area of social life explored here, even though our sample is not representative of "Australian women" in all their heterogenous groupings and settings.

At the same time, it should be noted that there was a degree of a social mix in our group of women (as indicated by their occupation, education and place of residence) and that most of them expressed similar concerns and shared a particular understanding of social representations of birth, motherhood and womanhood. This suggests the possibility of a basic experiential communality amongst women in society; it also reflects the fact that contemporary culture is not necessarily class specific, although particular experiences of any member of society may well be. These experiences can, of course, be variously mediated within specific institutional settings. However, the ways in which this mediation can occur is not, as suggested above, our main concern. In this book, our interest lies primarily in the cultural significance of birth and mothering and the manner in which this significance is individually and collectively represented.

Our data are clearly narrative and biographical in character. Although our focus is narrower than the life-history approach and the data are not presented in the case-study format, our treatment of them is consistent with their biographical character. In discussing the major themes that have emerged from interviews and observation, we identify relevant core categories in individual "story lines" (Strauss and Corbin, 1990). In the wide domain of actively structured everyday life (Bertaux and Kohl, 1984), such an approach is more productive than an orientation which conceptualises the actor (informant) as a point of intersection of macro-social forces, and is thus merely expressive of the operations of these forces. In this sense our interviews are more than a method of data-collection; they also constitute specific ways of addressing theoretical questions which seek to elucidate generalisations and in turn evaluate them by conceptual analysis rather than statistical intuition.

Following Silverman (1985), we hold that interviews are "displays of reality" which are indicators, in their content, of social and cultural elements giving "evidence of the perspective of a particular group" (Hammersley and Atkinson, 1983:106). This perspective, as argued above, is here conceptualised (admittedly somewhat loosely) as that of "Australian women". Consequently the first step in understanding what is displayed in the interviews is to locate their contents in a framework of the commonsense knowledge of everyday life we share with our informants.

RESEARCHING AMONG WOMEN

The interviewing method we used—multiple, in-depth interviews over a period of time—enabled us to build up a relationship with each woman who participated in the study. We shared our experiences of the life-events under investigation. Researching amongst women is always a personal matter, in the sense that the anonymous, objective, instrumental presence of the researcher cannot be realised in the context of interactions amongst women. This has been noted as a matter of fact by several investigators (e.g. Oakley, 1981; Finch, 1984); our own experience is certainly in accord with the contention that interviewing women (by women) generally involves, at the very least, becoming personally acquainted.

The shared structural position of being a woman appears to require "placement" of the interviewers in relation to the crucial categories of marriage and motherhood (Finch, 1984:78). In relation to our study, it seemed natural to volunteer personal details during the course of the (usually first) interviews. This happened more often spontaneously than deliberately, as an aspect of the atmosphere of trust and confidentiality which characterised our interviews and which, again, evolved naturally rather than by design. Of course, the informality and closeness of the relationship between woman interviewer and interviewee may occur as a consequence not only of being women, but also of employing ethnographic methods in one's own culture and in studying a subject that is intensely personal.[4] Technically speaking, then, we developed a great deal of "rapport" with our informants. Traditional textbooks on methodology recommend this (often together with "objectivity"), since it is seen to facilitate the flow of information to the researcher (Ackroyd and Hughes, 1981). However, it is not often acknowledged (but see McRobbie, 1982) that the congeniality between interviewer and interviewee, while expediting the data-collection process, can create the basis for an exploitative relationship which favours the researcher and makes it possible for her to take advantage of the situation for her own (research) ends in ways which go beyond the ostensible definition of the purpose of the interview. It is necessary to discuss these points in some detail.

A number of scholars have addressed the personal politics of social research, particularly in ethnographic fieldwork where the relationships between the researcher and the researched are both extensive and intensive (Golde, 1970; Pettigrew, 1981), but also in interviewing (Oakley, 1981; Roberts, 1981). Ann Oakley's discussion of her approach to and experience of interviewing in the collection of data for her study of transition to motherhood (Oakley, 1979; also Oakley, 1980 and 1981) is particularly relevant to us, since essentially we have covered the same ground and have used the same methodology: serial interviewing during

---

4. Along these lines, Siriporn Chirawatkul (1993) refers to her use of what she terms "self disclosure" to establish rapport and easiness with her research participants, in a study on menopause in northeastern Thailand; as she argues, the discussions (interviews and focus groups) could not have proceeded had she insisted on and maintained her status as outsider.

pregnancy and the first months of new motherhood. Here it is useful to detail the main points that Oakley makes with regard to feminist research and to reflect on the way in which we have dealt with like situations and events.

Oakley argues that interviewing protocol, as set out in basic methodology textbooks (e.g. Goode and Hatt, 1952; Selitz *et al.*, 1962; Galtung, 1967), fails to fit the practice of interviewing, at least when the interviewer is feminist and the people with whom she is working are women. In particular, she questions the viability and morality of the maintenance of the interviewer's anonymity, the limitations of the purely data-collecting function of the interviewer, and the definition of the interviewing relationship as basically instrumental "rapport". As defined in the texts, "rapport" is a superficial relationship aimed at setting the interviewee sufficiently at ease to begin to part with information. Related to this is an injunction on the two-way flow of information that might deflect the participants in the interview from its true purpose. A hierarchical relationship is established: the interview is orchestrated by the interviewer; the interviewee is expected to comply by proceeding with the interview, observing the content of the exchange and the order of issues to be discussed, and providing the interviewer with all the information that is sought. Oakley further comments on the concern with "bias" that might arise if the interviewer steps outside the interviewing brief, or moves into a relationship of friendship (Oakley, 1981:44-46). In reaction to this protocol, Oakley argues first, that the use of prescribed interviewing practice is morally indefensible; second, that there are general and irreconcilable contradictions in the textbook paradigm; and third, that finding out about people—the sociological purpose of interviewing—is best achieved when the relationship of interviewer and interviewee is symmetrical and the interviewer is prepared to invest personal identity in the relationship (Oakley, 1981:41).

OURSELVES IN THE PICTURE

Our own research on mothering also presented us with challenges to traditional notions of interview behaviour. The kind of relationship that we established with participants in this study inevitably and necessarily broke sociological convention. The subject matter of our research had much to do with this. Simply, we were inquiring into matters that were intensely private and personal, matters of emotion as well as of fact that could have been discussed only in a perfunctory and superficial manner had we held to a conventional model of sociological research method. We would have been uncomfortable maintaining the appropriate (but ill-defined) distance that ensured our "objectivity"; it is highly unlikely that our informants would have been so generous in welcoming our intrusions had we done so. In agreement with Oakley, we were not merely uncomfortable in maintaining a hierarchical relationship with our informants, but would have found it artificial to do so, since women do not usually deal with other women in positions of power and authority. At the same time, we were sensitive to a rather different relationship: we were dependent on the women who had volunteered their time, and were aware of the demands that we made on them. Both during pregnancy and after delivery, our informants were busy; sometimes they were under considerable stress or were tired; we had asked them to give time to provide us with both their descriptive account and the analysis of the process of becoming a mother. We encroached on their hospitality, very often interviewing them in their homes and accepting cups of tea in their kitchens. At the very least, we sought to minimise the inconveniences that we caused: to fit into their schedules, to help with dish-washing and to hang out wet nappies, and to nurse their infants as we pried into their lives.

As a matter of course we gave back information, both practical (e.g. regarding hospital procedure, breast-feeding, postpartum check-ups) and personal: our own reproductive histories were part of a shared exchange that characterised the interviews. The interviewing that took place did not lack direction as a result, but the atmosphere was one of warmth and friendship; we were interested, as persons, in the experiences of the women and in their infants who were central to this. With many informants, the one-sidedness of the relationship diffused: informants brought their new babies to our offices as a break in their routine; we chatted on the phone; we met for coffee to talk about their babies but not to conduct a formal interview. Lenore gave birth to her two children during the course of this research and thus her inter-actions with the women in the study took on another dimension: as a group of women with small children, we met for lunches, afternoon teas and birthday parties as the days of early mother-hood passed; in some cases we baby-sat and wet-nursed each others' infants to provide each other with brief breaks during the intense early weeks of mothering. In one case, too, the conventions of research were entirely set aside as Lenore intervened to facilitate professional advice and assistance to a mother who had given birth to a child with severe congenital abnormalities. Similarly, Mira formed friendships with some of the women, especially the older ones; having a shared past as adults during two decades or so of rapid social change, we enjoyed the joint exploration of develop-ments in the present of trends we had already sensed before. To some of our colleagues, this appeared highly unconventional soci-ology; to us, it seemed proper and appropriate that we minimise the hierarchy of researcher and research subject. It was, of course, personally rewarding to do so.

Women who participated in the study furthered our analysis through their own insights and theories of motherhood and moth-ering. They were also interested in what other women in the study thought, experienced and felt. Not only did our respondents seek practical and personal information, then, but also information concerning the "other mothers" and how they dealt with the crises of early mothering. "Our book" was a shared project,[5] its contents

---

5. This is to be taken at face-value. Here we are not suggesting—or "gesturing towards"—any commitment on our part to a methodology which assumes the necessary relativities of experience/conduct according to the context within which it is constructed, re-constructed or de-constructed, as the case may be (e.g. Weedon, 1987; or, from the point of view of "memory work", Haug, 1987).

seen as a manual to motherhood as well as a contribution to sociological research. To those women, we regret sincerely that this book has been so long in its appearance.

We have noted that our primary method was serial interviewing, with interviews often extending over some hours. But as stated before, this was supplemented by participant observation, accidental in so far as Lenore's pregnancies were not actually timed to coincide with the project. Yet this coincidence proved invaluable, providing us with the lived experience of the processes into which we were inquiring. Lenore took advantage of both pregnancies— in 1984 and 1986—to attend a wide range of classes: antenatal exercise and birthing education classes conducted by the Childbirth Education Association, Homebirth Association Education classes, and hospital-based parents' birth-classes and physiotherapy exercise classes. She also visited various health-professionals (general practitioners, obstetricians, nurses) and attended NMAA (Nursing Mothers' Association of Australia) support group meetings and larger functions. In addition, in 1987 she took on the role of partner/birth attendant through the pregnancy, labour and delivery of a close friend. This again allowed a new position from which to view and reflect on the processes of motherhood and childbirth. Each new involvement constituted a new layer of knowledge, understanding and caring. The role of reflexivity in this study is not to be underestimated: aspects our own biographies constituted a part of the social data with which we worked.

The reflexive component of our inquiry was considerably enhanced by our dialogue concerning our own experiences. With collaborative research and joint authorship it is understood, as a matter of course, that the exchange of ideas contributes to the processes of data collection and interpretation of findings and it goes almost without saying that this has been one of the advantages of our work together. But in addition, in our study, our own personal experiences and our empathic responses to our informants represented some of our subject-matter. We discussed these, and their significance for our research, both as women and as sociologists—inevitably so, as can be expected, on both counts. The insights derived within this process rendered our personal contributions to our study self-consciously, explicitly and critically subjective. In dialogue, we could see more clearly where our experiences were related to, or separated from, those of others—and where our understanding of personal situations and circumstances could be validly anchored to general analytic considerations.

QUALIFICATIONS AND REGRETS

Naturally all our interviewees were assured of the confidentiality of our procedures through all the usual safeguards, such as the use of pseudonyms and deletion of records. Nevertheless we felt overwhelmed at times by the intimate nature of the information given to us freely, without prompting, and wondered whether this had happened inadvertently, as the result of the emotional seductiveness of the interest and attention from us—or whether the information was entrusted to us with deliberation. We contemplated the first possibility with some unease and the second with gratitude, though we were clear that in either case some of the material which we obtained would not be used; at the very least, it would be insensitive on our part to use it. In most cases, this had no substantial consequences for our discussion, since, firstly, a great deal of this material was, in fact, not directly relevant to the themes being explored in this research; and secondly, as the research is conceptualised in terms of dimensions of experience, rather than within a framework of an analysis of associations between categories of events and circumstances across a number of "case-studies", an exhaustive inventory of all the reported material is not required. Thus it can be said that the selectiveness of our material and its use in an illustrative, rather than comprehensive, manner, protects our informants' feelings in a way which is, at the same time, methodologically consistent with the aims of this research.

Nevertheless, we need to acknowledge that such a procedure is depriving us of the opportunity to do justice to our informants in quite a different respect. Everyone's life is unique and remarkable, constituting as it does a totally individual pattern. It is therefore both diminishing and disrespectful to abstract from this pattern and use parts and aspects of it in a discussion the parameters of which preclude the possibility of demonstrating fully, in every case we have thus used, the internal cohesiveness and meaning of an individual life. Given the brief which we have formulated for this inquiry it is inevitable that we display the information from interviews in a fragmentary manner since it is only in specific actions and attitudes that particular social forces and structures intersect demonstrably with, and are constituted by, individual biographies. And yet, from a human point of view, we regret the shortcomings of our procedure and wish to apologise to the women with whom we worked for a cavalier treatment of their life-stories, however carefully this treatment may have been chosen for the task at hand.

INTERESTS AND REASONS

It is necessary for us to state all this, speaking as women researching amongst women. But there is no implication in these statements that epistemologically research by women concerning women can be distinguished from any other kind of social inquiry—nor that this kind of research is feminist research specifically for women. The "strong programme" in the feminist critique of social research implies not only the appreciation of gender relations as an explanatory category, but also the epistemological distinction of the "special skills"—for example, of "women's labour" (Rose, 1986) or "maternal thinking" (Ruddick, 1989)—that women bring to research. This is a distinction of form, rather than only of content, of merely contributing to social science analysis "second order constructs from experience" (Stanley and Wise, 1979) of being a woman. The inquiry into the everyday world is similarly seen to represent the special standpoint of women: "(A) sociology for women...(and) its analytic procedures must preserve the active and experiencing subject(s)...situated in the actualities of their everyday worlds" (Smith, 1988:105–106). However, much methodological writing which is not explicitly feminist has stressed the reflexive, contextual ("life-world") and personal factors in research (e.g. Ackroyd and Hughes, 1981; Silverman, 1985) that have been emphasised and claimed by feminist researchers. As well, women researchers' concerns with meaning and process have been part of social anthropology research for some time (Frankenberg, 1984) and can also be seen in classic sociological works (Thomas and Znaniecki, 1918). Thus we class our epistemological assumptions with those of qualitative social science research in general.

We hold that a social scientist who articulates women's experiences is not necessarily thereby creating a science for women, as Oakley (1981) would have it; rather, she is starting with the assumption that the subjective experience of anyone is significant—though, as a woman, she may choose to study the experiences of women. In doing so ourselves we acknowledge that social inquiry implies the recognition of a plurality of interests within the community (Barnes, 1979) and thus also amongst women (Crouch and Lovric, 1989). This plurality of interests and attitudes is reflected in our data and while we, as social researchers, look for trends and correspondences within these data, we are conscious of the need to keep the defining properties of our key concepts grounded in our material (Glaser and Strauss, 1967; Strauss and Corbin, 1990) rather than in any pre-existing assumptions we may, in fact, hold regarding the needs and inclinations of women as a category, or in any desire we may have to construct for us (women) "different lives in interaction with the world" (Harraway quoted in Rose, 1986). In other words, we have sought to be surprised by our data in preference to having our presuppositions confirmed by them. Therefore we have tried to avoid allowing our feminist concerns to be translated directly, as epistemological tools (Harding, 1984), into attitudes and judgements regarding our findings. In our own way, this stance conforms to the feminist philosophy of knowledge which requires "critical, self-reflexive methods...in order to block the intuitive, spontaneous conscientiousness of nature and inquiry to which all of us, but especially scientists, are susceptible" (Harding, 1991:309).

In the short run, nevertheless, our research has been "for women" in its very process—for those women with whom we worked, who thus became our friends, unburdened themselves to us, called on us for advice and help and commented on our interpretations and analysis. In the long run, we hope that our work will be of benefit to all women—women as actual, specific, individual persons acting in a complex world within which their needs and inclinations are only partially and selectively accommodated. In so saying, we place ourselves on the side of "good science" in its human/feminist context, even though we do not have an explicitly formulated—and basic to inquiry, according to Bhaskar (1989)— social theory of precisely why and how it is to be done. But we have tried, all the same. The chapters that follow give an account of our work, our thoughts and our feelings—and, in this way, of our philosophy, only one assumption of which needs to be stated here: any account of reality must be incomplete and partial, in both senses of the latter term. The dynamic and complex conditions of existence allow no alternatives. Nonetheless, these conditions do not necessarily preclude the possibility of validity for a given account, including ours.

PART TWO
BIRTH, THE CENTRAL ISSUE

Chapter 2

IMAGES OF BIRTH, PAST AND PRESENT

Becoming a mother is processual: it does not occur, in personal, social and cultural terms, with the moment of delivery. The process which incorporates the period of pregnancy, birth and the puerperium provides a woman with time to adjust to her changing status. During this time, she moves through a number of transitional phases, each contributing to the gradual development of her new social and personal identity as a mother. With delivery, the social status of motherhood is achieved, but the months that follow are no less essential for the woman's absorption of this new status, for the establishment of the relationship with her infant, or for the structuring of a new way of life in which to accommodate this relationship. Yet, in Australia as well as most other industrialised societies, the postpartum period is given no special attention. This is reflected in minimal structured care, usually marked only by a brief stay in hospital to ensure the health of the neonate and the beginning of the physical recovery of the mother, and by a perfunctory visit to the medical practitioner, usually an obstetrician, six weeks after giving birth. During this same period, weekly visits to a baby-health centre may commence where the attention is directed, generally speaking, towards the infant rather than the mother. Women cease to be of sustained professional interest once they have delivered successfully and have left the hospital grounds (Manderson, 1981:509).

In industrialised societies, the emphasis on pregnancy and birth is generally associated with the highest degree of medical management these processes can accommodate. The influences which can thus be exerted over the "outcome" can then also be used as an objective criterion of the efficacy of procedures employed to secure its positive qualities ("mother and baby both well"). Delivery is the high point of this period, the hours of labour and the event of parturition being the main focus culturally as well as physically. Pregnancy is a build-up to this crisis, its duration divided into trimesters not only on biological grounds and for medical purposes but also to allow the pregnant woman to prepare for birth and motherhood within a meaningfully calibrated period. Various markers can then appropriately be placed within this time-frame: the transition into maternity-clothes; the gradual acquisition of clothing and equipment for the baby; attendance at ante-natal classes; increasing visits to the doctor; registration at a maternity hospital; a tour of the labour ward etc. Not all women undertake all these "journeys" (Turner and Turner, 1978) in the same way, but all share a sense of anticipation, of approach to a singular and monumental event in their lives.

THE IMPORTANCE OF BIRTH

Not surprisingly, many activities during pregnancy centre on preparation for labour and emphasise the importance of a "good" birth. Through the increased public representation and discussion during the past decade or so—in books, magazines, and TV programs, for example—birth has come to be seen as something that can be done well or badly, an activity in which women might succeed or fail, not in terms of delivering a live and healthy infant but rather in terms of their own management and experience of it. As birth has become less common in a demographic sense since fewer children are born to women to-day than fifty or a hundred years ago (the fertility rate in Australia declined from 3.06 in 1947 to 1.85 in 1989), so it has gained importance culturally; simply, if a woman is to give birth once or twice only, she then seeks to perfect this singular event. Childbirth is, in Romalis' words (1981:10) a "performance defined by and enacted within a cultural context". In Australia, as elsewhere, it continues to be a central event which locates women with respect both to other women and to men, since for women, social adulthood is constituted not only in the completion of their education or in their work experience, but also by their becoming mothers (Rich, 1976:25; Michaelson, 1988a:2–4).[6]

Women's experiences of transition to motherhood cannot be understood—or even described—without an account of birth as the focus of social processes and cultural attitudes in relation to motherhood. Birth is regarded, in all societies, as the primal and most crucial "rite of passage" (van Gennep, 1960), since it is an event which brings about significant discontinuities: a new human being and thus also a new pattern in a human group; for the mother, the end of pregnancy and the beginning of nurturing— and for a *primipara*, in addition, a different status and a different way of being in the world. Birth is also universally perceived as an affirmation of—and a necessary condition for—the continuation of the patterns within which our lives are lodged and which ultimately ensure the lasting existence of our species. Psychoanalytic thinking suggests that the sexual and life-threatening aspects of parturition connect with both Eros and Thanatos in our Unconscious; "this, following Freud, implies that birth will be managed and controlled beyond the practical requirements of the occasion" (Crouch and Manderson, 1993). Along the same lines, though in somewhat different theoretical language, it can be said that birth blurs the boundaries between the sacred and the profane, thus signalling danger (Douglas, 1966) that is to be contained by whatever means the culture has in store.

The liminality of birth is also lodged in other contradictions it evokes: between nature and culture, the biological and the social,

---

6. It is in consequence of this, at least in part, that infertility remains an important social sin of omission.

illness and health, the unknown and threatening world within us and the familiar, everyday setting around us. At birth, these dichotomised realms are brought uncomfortably close together, while the differences between them are thrown into sharp relief by the circumstances of parturition itself—where there is always blood, pain and vulnerability, however controlled the situation may be and however domesticated and tamed its setting.

These circumstances endow the process of labour with the power, so to speak, of expressing symbolically important cultural themes through both the various aspects of the management of this process and the ideas which define the desirability of such management at any given time. The practical and the symbolic are thus interlocked and mutually reinforced in a context of historically developed practices and shared beliefs. Consequently a consideration of the changing images of childbirth in recent decades may provide the basis for a better understanding of the social and cultural forces which impinge, in the contemporary situation, on the experiences of new mothers.

THE FOETUS AND THE FAMILY

In the 60s, *Life Before Birth* by Ashley Montagu (first published in 1961) was a best-seller. In Chapter 15 ("The Bridge: Birth"), the author juxtaposes two propositions: "the most dangerous journey in life is through the four inches of the birth canal" and "none of the developments and changes which life brings find the individual so well prepared as for birth" (Montagu, 1967:221), and a dialectic relationship is then postulated between the conditions described by these two statements. Be that as it may, what is of interest here is the statements' dramatic emphasis which, we suggest, reflects the spirit of the two post-war decades when the main actor in the drama of birth was the foetus—the embodiment of the miracle of life, formed, in forty-one weeks, from invisibility to perfection, its spectacular entry into the world a process beset with potential hazards. For example "the child is being assaulted on all sides by the contracting uterus. His head is progressively pressed and squeezed against the walls of his mother's bony outlet. In addition, he may be having a hard time breathing oxygen" (Montagu, 1967:223); however, fortunately, "although his situation is fraught with uncertainty and discomfort, he is probably not conscious of pain…With his cries immediately after he is born, the child signals that he has survived the most difficult stage of his journey" (Montagu, 1967:223).

Historians of medicine have been able to supply the practitioners' versions of this view. For example, Shorter (1984) quotes from the 1966 edition of *Williams Obstetrics* "…the focus of obstetric thinking has been directed increasingly toward infant survival and the prevention of trauma to the child during birth" (Shorter, 1984:175); and (from the president of an obstetric association in the 1960s): "a change in attitude has occurred, formerly the focus was on the mother and delivery, and now it is centred on foetal outcome" (Shorter, 1984:175). This is not to say that the welfare of the mother was not deemed important; however, it was not, in the last analysis, the primary object of attention. Even with those who appeared to be particularly concerned with the woman's needs in labour, the foetus came first. In her introduction to *The New Childbirth*, a pregnancy and birth manual with a "natural childbirth" orientation, Erna Wright (1974:11) holds that "expectant parents can know that they need not be helpless in the face of the birth of their child, but can be partners in the team which ensures the safe arrival of the new member of the family". There is little doubt about the main focus of attention here.

The importance of the foetus in obstetric considerations was functionally associated with a growing tendency towards manipulation of various aspects of the labour process (Oakley, 1986b): the use of forceps, the lithotomy position, Caesarean delivery, induction, episiotomy—"sparing the baby's head the necessity of serving as a battering ram" (Shorter, 1984:172)—foetal monitoring and sundry antiseptic measures. The structural aspect of this orientation was expressed in the increasing presence and importance of the specialist obstetrician whose authority made it difficult for women to attain some measure of autonomy and control in the process of birth, hopes of which had previously glimmered when, around the 1920s, "progress in technique represented a deliverance from the horrors of traditional childbirth and opened up the possibility of pleasure in the birth experience unconstrained by fear of death or mutilation" (Shorter, 1984:176). Indeed, the availability of drugs to reduce pain in childbirth was originally also seen with this in mind (e.g. see Drake, 1902:35–36, 108–109).

The evolution of medical monopoly of obstetric practice—institutionally, professionally and ideologically[7]—has been discussed at length by other scholars (Ehrenreich and English, 1973; Oakley, 1975; Schloten, 1977; Jordan, 1978). It is important to note, however, that the development of obstetrics and the demise of traditional midwifery occurred not simply as an extension of professional control over women's bodies and women's work, but also in response to the real risks that childbearing had presented in the past. Women themselves, of course, had always been aware of the risks, but over and above the threat of death or mutilation for mother or child, there was pain—and it was largely because of women's desire to rid themselves from it that "the demise of midwifery and the resultant medicalisation of childbirth were consequences of forces within the women's community as well as from outside it" (Riessman, 1989:198). Thus the medical concept that represents pregnancy as hazardous and childbirth as life-threatening has had an empirical basis as well as an ideological dimension. Only in recent decades have the risks of birth diminished.[8] Significantly, however, it has been precisely during this period that medical and surgical intervention has increased as professional overseers of pregnancy and birth have sought to

---

7. The terms "ideology" and "ideological" have a broad field of connotations in sociology. Here we are using them in their general, "ordinary" sense: "ideology"—"a body of doctrine, myth and symbol of a social movement, institution, class, or large group...with reference to some political or cultural plan" (The Macquarie Dictionary, 1980).

8. For example, in New South Wales, maternal mortality dropped from 5.1 (per 1000 live births) in 1935 to 0.32 in 1963 (NSW Department of Health, 1965:54).

maintain their legitimate, scientifically buttressed control, in the face of growing criticism of that very control.

Shorter (1984) has traced the increasing importance of doctors in deliveries to the preferences of middle-class women, during the late nineteenth century, for fashionable and effective—in the control of pain and emergencies—operators. More recently, Mitford (1992) has documented the popularity of the "Twilight Sleep" anaesthesia in the United States throughout the 1920s and 1930s. While the relief of pain through improved anaesthetic procedures has played a major part in the rise in importance of the medical profession's role in labour, the growth of the hospital network and the improvements of the facilities contained within them provided the context for a concentrated display of professional expertise and the visible organisation of obstetric activity into a set of institutionalised practices. Hence the use of the term "management" in obstetric literature: pregnancy and birth were to be corralled into events that could be monitored, organised, manipulated and controlled in the same general manner as all other medical and surgical procedures.

The removal from labour of significant risk of injury, pain and death for the mother was not the only condition that shifted professional attention towards the foetus. The acceptance— socially as well as professionally—of labour as a process to be manipulated primarily towards a good foetal outcome was in itself at least partly the result of technical advances which made it possible to assess that outcome. In turn, "the obstetrical pursuit of more and more knowledge about the foetal conditions (became) integral to the obstetrical claim to expertise in general" (Oakley, 1986b:183). Feminist analysis has further suggested that medical practitioners have usurped women's bodies—as well as women's realm of competence—through the conversion, by superfluous interventions, of a natural process, i.e. birth, into an illness, a medical problem (Oakley, 1975).[9] This line of reasoning

---

9. More recent commentaries on further developments in this process of the "medicalisation" of women's bodies include those concerning conceptive technology, prenatal diagnosis, contraception, and the definitions and management of other female biological processes, including menstruation, menopause and breastfeeding. See for example, Crowe, 1985; Martin, 1987; Oakley, 1987; Stanworth, 1987; Rapp, 1988a and 1988b; Scutt, 1988; and Rowland, 1990).

continues the by now well-known history of "the 'capture' of pregnancy from midwives and its appropriation in the nineteenth
century by the burgeoning, male-dominated profession"
(Richman, 1987:66).

While plausible on several counts, such analyses impute institutional intentionality which is as difficult to substantiate as it is to
refute. In reality, we can expect the ascent of the medical/techno-
logical management of birth—and of its social acceptability—to
have been a complicated process in which a number of factors
have reinforced one another, in a manner similar, for example, to
the way in which the desire of the *nouveau riche* middle classes for
conspicuous consumption supported, during the nineteenth
century, the expansion of the medical profession by fostering the
image of frailty and invalidism of the genteel women during pregnancy (Rosengren, 1962). It is necessary, then, to consider broad
cultural trends of the times and their structural setting. In the
context of the present discussion, the "baby boom" era, with its
cultural ideal of family life, requires closer attention.

THE LUCKY COUNTRY

In Australia, as in the USA and the rest of the industrialised
"West", the period following World War II was the age of the
"marriage revolution" (Burns, 1983), witnessing a rise in the
number of marriages and their concentration in the early twenties
for women and late twenties for men. For instance, in Australia,
63.5% of men were married by age 29 in 1954 (43.9% in 1933)
and, in the same year, 59% of the women were married by age 24
(31.2% in 1933); it was estimated that 50% of women were
married by the age of 21 in 1955 (Burns, 1983). These marriages
were characterised by a companionate spouse relationship,
upward social mobility and a relatively smaller number of
children, the crude birth-rate, for example, dropping from 24.1 in
1947 to 22.5 in 1954 (Australia, 1984). Hence the "baby boom"
children were at the same time socially visible as a group, due to
numerous young marriages and consistently early childbearing

within them, and precious as individuals for each nuclear family of which they were such a significant part. A home and children by the age of thirty represented the ideal social norm—covertly oppressive of women though it was (Friedan, 1968)—and family life was portrayed as the most enjoyable aspect of existence. This spirit of "family renascence" (Berger and Berger, 1984) was facilitated by economic conditions of relative prosperity, high levels of employment and low interest rates, thus arising in an atmosphere of optimism and expansiveness.

Lees and Senyard (1987) argued that modernisation, already well under way for some time in the USA, came to Australia somewhat suddenly in the 1950s, with rapidly increasing urbanisation, mechanisation of most aspects of life and generalised consumerism in the American style. Australia had thus entered its "corporate urbanisation" phase (Mullins, 1988), the long-term structural and cultural ramifications of which were both extensive and varied, as well as often problematic (see, for example, Connell and Irving, 1980; also Kilmartin and Thorns, 1978). At the time, however, the new prosperity, the new cars and gadgets and the new open-plan homes (with L-shaped living areas, built-in kitchens and shower-recesses) made life easier and more comfortable and enhanced, it seems, the centrality and importance of family life, all the more satisfying as it went on amidst the new trappings of cosy domesticity: the refrigerators, cake-mixers, vacuum-cleaners, venetian blinds and drip-dry pink and blue toddlers' play-suits flapping on the faithful Hills clothes-hoist proudly positioned in the middle of the sunny, well-groomed buffalo grass lawn.

The image of women as emotional, dependent and nurturing wives and mothers, lodged in cosy domesticity, was forged in the wake of capitalism's drive for increasing consumption (Ehrenreich and English, 1973). Science (and medicine) buttressed the sexual romanticism of "keeping the home fires burning" by rendering rational and appealing the efforts to maintain personal, domestic and emotional hygiene. This trend superseded—or rather, incorporated—the earlier "modernising" drive towards greater efficiency

in the home.[10] Women were perceived as being immersed in vacu-
uming, refrigerating, deodorising, getting rid of "germs in the
home" with all the new "laboratory-tested" cleansers and household antiseptics, as well as in intensive mothering in the light of
research on maternal deprivation (Bowlby, 1953) that had begun
to trickle into Australia in the 50s (Reiger, 1986). Works dealing
with the psychology of motherhood (and "proper mothering")
provided the ideological justification for women to be engaged in
full-time parenting. In Australia this was fostered by a national
need for an increased population that was to be met in the short
term by the slow liberalisation of immigration laws, and in the
longer term by encouraging reproduction. Motherhood was in the
national interest; and full-time mothering ensured the emotional,
mental and physical well-being of each new child.

Thus Australian women, like women in other industrialised
countries during the post-war period, led their largely domestic
lives in a manner which, they could believe, was both feminine and
modern. The perception of labour—parturition—as a manageable, technically improved process, directed and manipulated
towards a maximally "good foetal outcome", fits intelligibly into
this context of meaning. The embryo,[11] with its miraculous and
yet predictable growth and development, may have been both a
meaningful, appealing image to the young couples of the post-war
era and a symbol of their aspirations, a metaphor for the
progress-oriented philosophy of their society.

The idea of progress was also quite centrally associated with the
philosophy and practice of medicine, securely based, as it was seen
to be, in science and its inexorable forward march. This notion was
comfortably supported by visible successes, e.g. the discovery and
development of antibiotics, the discovery of cortisone, the appli-
cation of radio-isotopes in medical research and diagnostic procedures, the Salk vaccine, and so on (Williams, 1975). Confidence

---

10. For a detailed discussion of this, see Rybczynski (1986).
11. The embryo was made publicly visible through exceedingly popular (at
the time) photographic works such as Lennart Nilsson's *A Child is Born*
(1965) (reproduced in *Life* magazine in the same year).

in increasing technical competence and the consequent manageability of all aspects of labour seemed to be the dominant spirit in obstetric practice. In the words of an Australian professor of obstetrics: "'difficult' is a comparative term; it will be used less frequently as the years pass and experience grows. Less frequently, too, will defeat be accepted with the words 'everything that's humanly possible has been done'" (Mayes, 1954).

It is from this time that we can date "heroic" medicine in obstetrics. Since the 1950s many new developments have taken place and in this process methods of controlling labour have interacted with foetus-oriented ante-natal care, each reinforcing the other. Thus:

> ...safe induction of labour is facilitated by methods of surveying fetal condition *in utero*, because the state of the resulting baby can be known, not just intimated. But, in turn, the knowledge gleaned from foetal monitoring may increase the urgency for a safe induction technique. The technique of inducing labour with oxytocic drugs has also directly spurred the need for new or improved labour technologies, for instance, the development of foetal heart-rate monitoring (Oakley, 1986b:209).

In the 1980s, this had developed to refinements such as amniocentesis, chorionic villus biopsy, epidural analgesia, sophisticated ultrasonics in the investigation of foetal states, and the use of various biochemical procedures for the determination of features of the maternal physiological environment (Adams, 1983; Rapp, 1988a and 1988b; Rothman, 1988).

SEEDS OF DISCONTENT

Thus obstetric technology diversified, became more efficient and more widely used. But since the early 70s, at least, strong criticism has been directed towards the "medical model" of birth (Haire, 1973; Arms, 1975; Oakley, 1975) and considerable public debate emerged over women's experiences of childbearing. Already in the 1960s, dissatisfactions began to be voiced with routine obstetric

procedures which were seen to be dominated by male professionals (Kitzinger, 1962); as early as 1958, *The Ladies Home
Journal* in the United States published "an avalanche" of letters
from readers voicing disappointment and anger in relation to
medical delivery procedures (Mitford, 1992:62). The upsurge of
criticism that followed had its sources in feminism on one hand,
and on the other, in the social movements of the late 60s and early
70s which were characterised by a general rejection of science and
technology, or rather of the privilege of technology over humanity.
Writers such as Navarro (1976) and Illich (1976) were critical of
the western hospital-based medical system and condemned the
increasing use of costly high technology and drugs in preference to
preventive medicine and health promotion—the more natural and
in the long run more productive and egalitarian alternatives. In
addition, Illich's work emphasised the dependencies and powerlessness created by science and technology, in medicine as much,
if not more, as in other fields (Albury, in press).

Such ideas began to have an impact in Australia against a background of rapid and complex social changes that had been under
way since the end of World War II. The increasing importance of
secondary industries, urbanisation, increase in "white collar"
workers' numbers (as well as their relative proportion in the
work-force) (Sinclair, 1980), the growth of the public service
bureaucracy, the proliferation of new professional and occupational groups, especially in various "services" (financial, education, health, social, research) and increasing consumerism—all
these constituted the new social world of the maturing
baby-boomers, easing their way into a now much larger and better
educated middle-class (Encel, 1978) in a newly affluent society.
Little experience of the country—the "outback"—and its hard-
ships remained in the lives of the average person in the 1970s,
whose consciousness was formed within a technological, consum-
erist, urban and bureaucratised environment. The growing
number of individuals (from 27 000 in 1951 to 108 600 in 1969)
attending tertiary education (Australia, 1970) began to pave the
way for a more self-conscious orientation to life, in the context of
an increasing tendency towards public social commentary that

was both provoked and secured by the relative prosperity of the times. During this period the position of women was affected by the changing circumstances of the period in a complex fashion (Mathews, 1984). A significant aspect of this was the fact that personal life "became the target for creating needs to be fulfilled with commodities" (Mathews, 1984:90), causing a shift in the content of femininity, a change which was "inevitably, contradictory. While woman in the home was the target of family-consumption advertising, increasingly more women had to earn regular wages to pay for the commodities. While woman partly separated from home was the target for personal advertising, increasingly more women took the quest for independence and self-fulfilment beyond the realm of the marketplace into political action" (pp. 90–91). Not surprisingly, the purely womanly activity of childbearing became a focus for both consumer demands and political action. As O'Brien (1981) has pointed out, production and reproduction both have their internal dynamics which, however, interact with one another. The advent of effective contraception has drastically altered women's reproductive relations in providing the material base for a new reproductive consciousness—but this consciousness has inevitably also been influenced by aspects of the social relations of production as these impinged on patterns of reproductive activity (and *vice versa*).

BEARING DOWN ON DOCTORS

The feminist critique of the "medical model" of birth developed around the notion of the colonisation of women's bodies by the medical profession. Enhanced and informed by the more broadly based objections to this model in general, it eventually crystalised in an attack on obstetric practice along two main lines: a) that many modern obstetric (male-doctor dominated) procedures were employed unnecessarily and to the detriment of the mothers' (and sometimes infants') well-being;[12] and b) that the whole

---

12. In this connection, it is instructive to note that Jessica Mitford (1992) has documented appalling treatment of women in labour wards in the Soviet Union—where the majority of doctors is female.

context and tenor of the medical mode of parturition were at variance with the essential, "natural" experience of labour and therefore with the real needs of birthing women (e.g. Tew, 1986; Thomas, 1986). Springing from these views, alternative approaches to birth have gradually become organised and institutionalised, emphasising, as their leading ideology, the normality and spontaneity of labour and focusing their activities around the concepts and practices of natural childbirth.

The concept of natural childbirth is not altogether new. Drake, writing in 1902, was already arguing the naturalness of pregnancy and childbirth, and minimisation of pain in labour through adherence to a regime of exercise, diet and appropriate state of mind. However, the ideas of Dick-Read (1942; also Dick-Read 1950, 1955)[13] on preparation for labour during pregnancy and the control of the fear of pain were most influential over a number of decades. Dick-Read was basically conservative and puritanical: childbirth without fear, according to him, was a matter of attaining an ideal, rather than a matter of personal autonomy and comfort for the mother. "The fearless woman advances to the dais of the Almighty to receive the prize for her accomplishment. She does not cringe in anticipation of admonition, but is proud and grateful for her just reward" (Dick-Read, 1968:31). In addition, Dick-Read also stressed that the ultimate knowledge and authority lay with the supervising and attendant medical practitioner. By contrast, the adherents of the more recent natural birth movement emphasise the right of a woman to do birth in a physical and social environment that offers her comfort and support rather than technology and efficiency, as well as—and more significantly (and politically), perhaps—an active and controlling role in the process. This position, at one edge, logically argues for the superiority of home rather than hospital as the appropriate place in which to give birth.

---

13. Dick-Read's writing about "natural birth", and the "unbelievable joy" of women who give birth naturally (1950:2) emphasises exercise and dietary prescription. For a discussion of the history of ideas, and the impact of Dick-Read and Lamaze on the natural childbirth movement, see Tanzer and Bloc, 1976.

There is a sharp contrast, then, between perceptions of the "medical model" and accounts of the alternative positions which have developed in opposition to it. The debates that have ensued about the particular aspects of the maternity services and obstetric practices occur as a part of a wider debate about the "medicalisation" of childbirth, of what Comaroff calls "the competing paradigms of pregnancy" (Macintyre, 1977). Within the paradigm of natural birthing, pregnancy and childbirth are regarded as positive and fulfilling experiences to be controlled by women and medical assistance is seen as a minimal insurance against possible complications. During pregnancy and in labour, the woman enjoys an egalitarian relationship with the practitioners who attend to her (including the medical professionals, if any) and whose intervention is minimal.[14] In the medical paradigm, pregnancy and labour are seen as processes akin to illness. Passively subject to experts' instructions, women cede control to the medical professionals, remaining relatively ignorant of their decisions. Childbearing is dangerous; medical assistance and intervention are uniformly necessary; the physical experiences of childbirth, perceived negatively, are to be alleviated or removed from consciousness wherever possible (Macintyre, 1977).

Both of these models, the "medical" and the "natural", represent ideal-typical formulations of attitudinal dimensions which are, in reality, distributed variously amongst women (Klee, 1986), as well as practitioners and hospitals[15]. The successful advocacy of natural birth over the past decade or so has led to significant

---

14.   Interestingly enough, the natural birth lobby has not objected to a number of pre-and post-delivery technological procedures (amniocentesis, ultrasound, chorionic villus biopsy, as well as regimes to sustain small birthweight babies). On the other hand, the cry "let Nature take its (her?) course" has been voiced more recently in relation to reproductive technology which is seen to have challenged, again, women's control of reproduction (Rowland, 1988) and feminine conceptualisations of motherhood (Rowland, 1991).

15.   For example a study of five teaching hospitals in Sydney (Hewson *et al.*, 1985) has shown wide ranges across institutions in practices such as forceps delivery 29%–51%, Caesarean births 2.5%–14%, spontaneous birth 44%–61% and episiotomies 59%–75.6%; also stirrups 16.5%–54% and no anaesthesia 8%–16%.

changes in general attitudes towards, and practices in relation to, birth. Alternative birthing centres have been established in association with an increasing number of hospitals and doctors' practices; conventional labour wards have been redecorated in a somewhat less sterile fashion—in visual accordance with rather stereotyped notions of a woman's bedroom (for example, with floral wallpaper)—and there has been increasing liberalisation of hospital policies and doctors' attitudes with regard to the way in which women may do birth. Hence the provision of bean-bags and squatting frames, the encouragement of partners, children and other "support persons" to be present at birth, the reduction of "prepping" procedures such as enemas and shaving of pubic hair, and the availability of labour options such as the Lamaze method,[16] or the assistance of midwives rather than specialist obstetricians. It appears that "many doctors have now accepted the consumers' distaste for unnecessary technological intervention" (Harkness, 1986).

At the same time there has been an increase in the popularity of, and support for, home birth. Although the numbers of women in Australia delivering at home have been small (1135 in 1985) (Dowrick, 1986), public attitudes have shifted markedly towards home and other alternative ways of doing birth. This is reflected in a growing number of newspaper and periodical articles criticising "medicalised" hospital birth and supporting natural and home births, as well as in the increased availability of books intended to assist women to give birth "naturally", with as little obstetric intervention as possible (see for example Brook, 1976; Kitzinger, 1979; Ewy and Ewy, 1982; Balaskas, 1983). Thus women (or, rather, activists on behalf of "women in general")—along with the popular press that may be taken to represent their views—have increasingly championed and demanded unanaesthetised

---

16. The ideas of Lamaze (1970) [1958] follow on from Dick-Read, and describe birth as a "moment of ecstatic fulfilment that the doctor should not take away from a woman" (Michaelson, 1988a:5). He advocates the father's sharing in birth as a means of supporting (middle-class) ideas of togetherness in marriage.

"natural" childbirth, in which the mother is a conscious participant in the management of the delivery.

Albury (in press) has suggested that this approach has over
recent years become incorporated into obstetric procedures which
are characterised now by preparatory training of the patient before
birth and active collaboration of the patient and medical personnel
during labour. These, in turn, as Albury further points out, render
the woman's subjectivity a central feature of the medical process.
Indeed, the phenomenological centre, the focus of contemporary
obstetric practice (perhaps especially for private patients), is the
mother—her body, her feelings, her preferences; in sum, her total
experience. While the foetus increasingly becomes the main object
of attention for various investigative procedures during pregnancy,
in labour the attention has shifted from the foetus to the mother
who is now the *dramatis personae* of this significant event. This is
not merely a change of focus from one object to another; it also
involves a shift of emphasis from outcome to process, from the
climax of the finale of parturition to effective choreography
throughout the whole performance during labour. This shift
concerns the actions and attitudes of the practitioners as much as
it does those of their clients.

WOMANHOOD TO THE FORE

Increasingly health care is seen as a commodity; the patient is both
"client" and "consumer". With birth, the eventual delivery of the
product (i.e. "mother and baby both well") has, by and large, been
established as not being seriously in doubt any more. During
recent decades, our collective social expectations have absorbed
general knowledge concerning the trends in this regard, such as
the significant decline in maternal and infant mortality. In
addition, lately prenatal diagnostic procedures have opened up the
possibility of having positive knowledge of important factors
where previously uncertainty prevailed. It is therefore now
possible—perhaps even necessary in face of the (paradoxically)
increased technological intervention during pregnancy (Corea *et
al.*, 1985; Stanworth, 1987)—to proclaim desirable those aspects

of the labour process which can be rendered significant through their associations with dispositional and emotional factors and thus make them into commodities. In the current mode of birth— the "natural", "holistic" approach—this new emphasis has shifted the apparent locus of control from the activities of the birth-attendants to the mother's body and feelings, thus securing for her the commodities of autonomy and authenticity. The woman's reactions take the lead in the sequence of events and her experience is unadulterated by mechanical or chemical (man-made?) interferences. On one hand, then, client satisfaction has been secured. On the other hand, however, a subtle moral dimension has been heeded, since there is a sense in which one can interpret the current features of the "good", mother-centred birth as observances of a requirement of procedural purity that is analogous to the uncompromising attitude towards antisepsis of the older, foetus-centred model of labour management.

It is suggested here that such procedural prescriptions and proscriptions—desirable, practical or necessary as some of them may be—are the underpinnings of fundamental moral principles concerning birth. Morality is always an issue with birth, because, as argued above, birth is a rite of passage, a transitional, liminal and therefore questionable phase of existence. As such, it must be "hedged about with ritual" (Leach, 1976:35), thus expressing significance beyond the pragmatic aspects of the event. Increasingly since the late 1970s, this rite of passage has been overlayed with more meaning in relation to the mother than has been the case previously. Salient social and cultural changes have brought this about.

Until relatively recently, motherhood was an ubiquitous phase of every woman's life-trajectory in principle, even if she actually remained childless and thus judged barren[17]. The family of the

---

17. Post World War II, childbearing was regarded as the means by which a couple became a family. Thus Ewy and Ewy (1982), for example, argue that childbirth is not "the birth of a baby, but the birth of a family" (p.24) and represent the involvement of the father as a means of promoting "mutual closeness and appreciation...childbirth is often the first meaningful challenge a young couple has to face. If the experience of childbirth is met with control and dignity, the husband and wife emerge with new confidence" (p.16).

"baby boom" era was the centre of a woman's existence; women "were to find their mission at home, as mothers and as the intelligent, sensitive companions to their husbands" (Berger and Berger, 1983:25). For the present generation, motherhood is rather more a question of choice and therefore a deliberate and self-conscious commitment. While previously all women were considered potential mothers but in the context of marriage only, since at least the 1980s women—single, married, with jobs or not, teenage, lesbian, middle-aged—might resolve, at a certain point of their lives and for a variety of reasons, to "have a child". Impressionistically, "having a child" seems to be a far more common figure of speech now than "starting a family", a phrase in habitual use during the post-war decades. If "having a child"—*now*—might represent an existential moment for an individual woman, this moment would have for her a particular set of meanings and be experienced differently from "starting a family"—*then*—which, while also subject to personal deliberation, was much more in the nature of relatively predictable participation in a socially defined institutionalised practice.[18] Since childbearing and childcare are no longer viewed as a taken-for-granted part of a woman's life-cycle, anxiety lurks in the shadows of the question of whether or not to mother—or "what sort of context for mothering one wants and deems essential" (Kaplan, E.A. 1992:182).

Thus it is not surprising that birth now is understood mainly as an important personal experience for the woman whose being it transforms so radically in so individualistic a set of circumstances. Procreation may indeed be "an episode in a woman's life, instead of a career" (Borrie as quoted in Edgar, 1981:17), but it is precisely this episodic nature that singles out the significance of

---

18. These trends are not limited to Australia. In the UK and USA also, marriage and childbearing have been postponed over recent decades, and in both cases, as in Australia there has been an increase in births out of wedlock and an increase of childlessness (see for example Toliver, 1986 and Kiernan, 1988). A study undertaken in Germany, concerned with the same trend in delayed marriage and motherhood, associates this with increased education rather than women's work/career (Blossfield and Huinink, 1991).

childbearing for the identity of the contemporary woman.[19] Understandably then also, significant persons are on hand to witness, celebrate and guard the ritual event and to secure the continuation of the social context within which the transformation is taking place. The physical closeness, holding of hands, massaging and so on, maintain the social personhood of the birthing mother and at the same time negate any "unnatural" instrumental components that may creep into the situation and threaten to contaminate it. The only intrusive technology allowed consists of cameras, tape-recorders and VCRs, extensively used to record and reify the event.

Birth, then, has considerable social significance; it has always represented more than a "bridge" from foetal state to person state for the neonate. The argument here has been that significant social themes are reflected in both the procedures and images of birth and that therefore these alter as social circumstances change, although this relationship is often obscured by the fact that the images are a mix of elements relating to both surface and realistic, as well as deep and symbolic, aspects of parturition. In connection with this point, it is important to consider the shift in feminist thought that has occurred in the past fifteen years or so. "Motherhood and domesticity having been negatively appraised, we re-valued them. And so with the wrongs nominally righted, the way was open for the positive aspects of womanhood to be rediscovered" (Mitchell, 1986:44). From the 80s on, much of contemporary feminism exalts in the specifically female qualities, celebrating "women's difference that is a source of richness and creativity" (Eisenstein, 1991:100) and fostering the awareness of the woman's natural self and its potential, including "the body and its reasons" (Salleh, 1981). This has been reflected very poignantly in contemporary images of birth, the quintessential female act,

---

19. This argument rests on our interpretation of a variety of sources from both sociological literature and various public media, as well as from general observation. It has not been derived primarily from our interview material, though it has been inspired by it in the sense that a discussion of the broader social and cultural context is necessary in order to bring out sociological significance of this material.

suggesting strongly that not only feminist theory, but also feminine awareness in general—in fact, the level of total cultural sensitivity—has been significantly altered in relation to issues of feminine identity and the social meaning of motherhood.

As womanhood acquires significance in its own right—rather than being a pre-condition for motherhood traditionally or, more recently, a gender-complex to be overcome (e.g. Firestone, 1970)[20]—motherhood has become an expression of it, symbolically represented by labour. Thus the experience of birth is valued and emphasised as the ultimate proclamation of a fully developed natural state, rather than as the beginning of a naturally fulfilling social career. But in the present cultural *milieu*, this enhanced esteem for the labour experience can have additional functional value: it can counterbalance the reduction of women's investment of time and energy in the activities associated with mothering in the long term, as increasingly women enter—and re-enter—the work-force and invest both physically and emotionally in the public sphere. In this view, "the fashionable lust for instantaneous 'bonding'" (Maynard, 1986), which forms a significant aspect of the "good birth" experience, may represent an attempt to secure through ritual intensification the instant accomplishment of the condition of attachment that cannot any more be assumed to exist *a priori*.

By the 1980s, then, birth imagery had become an integral aspect of a new feminine awareness and of a new sensitivity towards feminine identity in relation to the whole of the social world. It is against this background that we discuss women's actual experiences of birth in the chapter that follows.

---

20. Shulamith Firestone (1970) associated reproduction with subordination and argued for its separation from women as a precondition to liberation.

Chapter 3

TIMELY DELIVERIES: WOMEN AND MEN IN LABOUR

We begin this chapter with Pamela's story, selected for its apparently uneventful and normal course which, nevertheless, indicates the complex and problematic circumstances surrounding birth and labour in our time.

Pamela was 28 when first interviewed and had been married for four years. A forthright young woman, she speaks with a broad Australian accent, refers to her husband by his nickname, has a good eye for funny situations and a ready laugh to go with it; these temper her seemingly no-nonsense approach to life. She is a school-teacher and lives in a country town. During her pregnancy Pamela took "a reasonable amount of care": she ate healthy food, went for long walks and attended childbirth classes provided by Parents' Centres Australia. She thought these were very good, but after a while she worked out her own exercise program and continued with it by herself. There were no anxieties about the birth and no worries about the possibility of an episiotomy. Pamela did not prepare her perineum in any way as she felt that "you are either one who will tear it or you aren't". She never thought of the possibility of a home-birth—"not that I am against them, I just didn't think about it".

Pamela had intended to give birth in a squatting position. Upon hearing about this, Dr. C. (Pamela's obstetrician) laughed, saying he did not know what that meant. Pamela got up on the examination table, hitched up her skirt and demonstrated (she had witnessed several squatting births in Fiji—this having convinced her of the appropriateness of the method). Dr. C. said that the position would prevent him from seeing the direction of the baby's approach or whether an episiotomy was needed—though, he added, it probably would be anyway, this being the first baby. They agreed on a compromise: Pamela would half lie down, with knees bent and lean back a bit against a wall. Dr. C. also stated that he preferred pudendal blocks when giving an episiotomy, but Pamela said that she would want a local anaesthetic.

Pamela thinks Dr. C. is good. "If you go in with a list of questions he will spend time answering them and makes sure you are satisfied before you leave. But if you have no questions, then he does his routine, pats you on the head and says goodbye." The pregnancy proceeded uneventfully. Around the end of normal term, contractions started late one night. Mistaking them for a gastric attack after a meal in a restaurant, Pamela waited; as the pains became more frequent, she began to time them and when they occurred every two minutes, she woke her husband and they drove to the hospital, arriving there about 7.30 am. The midwife examined her and pronounced her "ready to go". In the labour ward, Pamela squatted on the bed ("Oh you're the one" the midwife reportedly exclaimed "we've heard a lot about you!").

By the time Dr. C. arrived at 9.15 am. ("I kept asking when he would get here because I felt I was waiting for him to let go"), she had numb legs from prolonged squatting and found it difficult to get into the position required for Dr. C. to be able to see properly the already crowning head; however her husband and a male nurse supported her body on each side and this helped her a lot. When the doctor arrived "everything was well on the way—two pushes and that was it!" although "I really needed a cut because his (the baby's) head was so big and I was so small...by that stage when he cut me it was a real relief...just didn't have time for all the drugs and all that...". Pamela was happy about the role played by nurses and midwife: "they did not break my waters—you do get told in these (childbirth) classes that (in hospital) they'll do this and they'll do that without asking you...They were terrific, all the way through, so encouraging...".

During the final stage of her labour Pamela became somewhat over-ventilated due to too frequent panting; the midwife corrected this and Pamela felt reassured. Throughout her labour the only thing she did not feel secure about was the pushing—she was not confident whether she had "got it right about the pushing and breathing bit—using the breath properly or wasting it". With the doctor's arrival, however, everything appeared to fall into place, so to speak. Pamela's husband told her afterwards, she reported with some emphasis, that a change came over everyone when Dr. C. came in, "it was as though he (Dr. C.) said 'come on, it's over'— and it really was".

Pamela spoke fondly, though not in over-emotional language, about the first contact with her baby son and his first sucks at her breast, remembering well that it was on the left side—and that she absolutely insisted on giving the right breast "a go" as well, getting her way here in the face of the opposition from the nursing staff, evidently almost equally determined to whisk the baby away to be "properly cleaned up and checked". She was happy to concede that there was a reason for this haste—"a lady about to deliver twins outside the door (of Pamela's delivery room) was busting to get in".

Later, in the ward with a cup of tea, she felt "very down" without the baby and asked several times, without much success, to have him brought to her. She thought that the four-hourly feeding routine was "silly" and eventually went to the nursery herself.

Pamela's story is, in many respects, quite a typical one for a number of women we have interviewed. So is her cheerful, practical manner of accepting "the bad and indifferent with the good and the very good", as one woman put it, although some of Pamela's actions also indicate a degree of rebellious determination to have her own way on certain matters. Along similar lines, these women were critical of some aspects of management of their labours; however, in general, they accepted these shortcomings as relatively unimportant and were content with the end-result.

Like Pamela, this group of women also liked and respected their doctors and had confidence in them; similarly, they were generally satisfied with the midwives and the nursing staff, the occasional specific complaint notwithstanding. As in Pamela's case, the mode of birthing was usually an eclectic mixture of approaches, with significant variations from woman to woman which clearly depended as much on ideas and practices favoured by institutions and practitioners as they did on the preferences of the women themselves. More often than not—as evidenced in Pamela's account—a degree of negotiation determined what would take place during labour.

It is instructive to consider what was negotiated in the case of Pamela, as well as what circumstances she thought noteworthy enough to point out to us. The squatting position was obviously something for which Pamela had to fight. The question of an epidural did not arise, as things worked out, but, all the same, Pamela had had a difference of opinion with her doctor over that matter. There was also the question of contact with the baby immediately after the birth, as well as access to him afterwards. All these issues point to the awareness, on Pamela's part, of the more "natural" aspects of childbirth currently favoured by an increasing number of women but not, as we have seen, by all doctors or nursing staff.

It is also of interest to note that Pamela did not specifically mention that her husband had been present at the birth—the information was given incidentally by pointing to the particular circumstance where his assistance had been necessary. This would suggest to us that his presence was unremarkable, taken for granted both by Pamela and her attendants. As far as the attitudes of the hospital and the doctor are concerned, we can glean here a situation where traditional medical beliefs and practices prevail but where, at the same time, innovative elements are allowed, either by negotiation with "the patient", or routinely.

Similarly, we can surmise that even women like Pamela, who live away from the city where "trends" are sharply visible in the context of highly urbanised everyday life, are attracted to modish ideas concerning the right way to do birth. They may go along with what happens to be available to them in the way of obstetric practice, but nevertheless press for, where possible, their personal choice of procedures associated with "natural", "unassisted" labour.

We have considered Pamela's story at the start of the chapter because the main discussion which follows below needs to be anchored to this story's most general theme—one which is echoed, in various ways, in the birth-stories of almost all other women we have interviewed. The theme—with its variations—represents, on the one hand, women's perceived need for, or at least knowledge of, the popularly understood benefits of natural birth practices, and, on the other, the accompanying harmonisations they try to achieve, both psychologically and practically, between the central cognitive *motif* of the "good birth" and their own particular circumstances. This generalisation is conceptually rather than statistically derived; it is based on the centrality and importance of this theme in our informants' accounts, as well as on its resonances with significant collective images.

DOING BIRTH THE RIGHT WAY

We have already contrasted the medical and the natural models of birth as ideal-typical representations of opposing tendencies. In reality, this opposition is resolved in eclectic mixtures of attitudes and actions; the ideal types can thus be conceptualised as dimensions of the *praxis* of birth. Different specific situations, both personal and institutional, private and professional, can then be located along each dimension, the point of intersection varying from case to case. Of course, we oversimplify again, as each dimension is associated with its own set of practical and ideological advantages. The medical dimension is securely lodged in intellectual, institutional and organisational frameworks and can therefore claim legitimacy as well as change adaptively without loss of identity. On the other hand, the "natural" model formulates a radical shift and therefore has novelty value; furthermore, the substance of the innovations resonates with many other broad, liberating, "anti-establishment" contemporary social movements which include, specifically, the women's movement. Most important for the present discussion, however, is the fact that it is also evangelical and prescriptive. The prescriptions are subtle since they do not consist of rules formulated through authority, but rather of imperatives implicit in the appropriation of assumptions regarding the naturalness, spontaneity and creativity of experience—and of women's rights to such experience.

The popular literature, including recent publications which deal generally with pregnancy and birth as well as those that explicitly advocate natural birth, provides a wealth of examples of the moral tone of the language which connotes ecstasy, triumph and creativity. For instance:

> It is worth pausing to remember that giving birth is one of the most marvellous and exciting experiences of your life. If there is pain, it isn't like other pain. For one thing you know the reason for it and that it won't go on for ever. For another, and quite unlike other pain, it has a purpose—there is a wonderful creative outcome at the end of it all (Blackie, 1986:94).

Articles in the Australian press are of particular interest because of their ideological cast. In advocating natural childbirth, labour that has involved the use of drugs or has concluded with manual assistance or surgery has been presented consistently in a negative light. One article (Lewis, 1984), for example, juxtaposed a Caesarean delivery and subsequent hospitalisation of the mother with a conventional hospital delivery without intervention, a home birth of twins and a delivery at a birth centre, the latter three marked by joy and ease. Of the Caesarean delivery, "'It was a mess. I was shocked, full of pain killers which I was allergic to...I couldn't sleep. I was over-tired and the next day I was in shock. I couldn't even put a sentence together. It got more and more terrifying...'. The next thing she knew she was in a psychiatric hospital" (Lewis, 1984:1–2). In contrast, the home birth, though a forty hour labour, was marked by a sense of control and confidence; the report of the hospital birth without intervention includes, of the crowning, that it was an "amazing" delivery: "The midwives were so in tune with what was happening to my body. It was all very gentle...the lights were kept very dim and everyone spoke softly" (ibid.).

Other articles emphasise the impersonal nature of a hospital environment, referring, for instance, to the "battery-hen atmosphere of hospital-oriented obstetrics" (Clarke, 1984) and, in advocating home birth, stress dislike of hospitals by the pregnant women; they also include implicit—and sometimes explicit—criticism of women who accept technological or chemical intervention: "She was exhausted, finding it difficult to concentrate on the contractions. If she had been in hospital it is quite likely that she would have been given drugs at that stage to ease the pain. *But she rallied*" (Rice, 1984; emphasis in the original).

Evaluative comments of this nature are backed up by direct criticisms of the practices associated with the medical model; we note with interest the quasi-scientific cast of these criticisms. Thus the Newsletter of a Sydney-based homebirth association, in a three-part condensed presentation of Haire (1973), argued that "there is gathering scientific evidence that the unphysiological lithotomy position...which is preferred by most physicians because it is more convenient for the accoucheur, tends to alter the normal foetal environment and obstruct the normal processes of childbearing, making spontaneous birth more difficult or impossible" (Homebirth Access Sydney, 1982:9). And: "In the light of the current shortage of qualified anaesthetists and anaesthesiologists and the frequent scientific papers now being published on the possible hazards resulting from the use of regional and general anaesthesia it would seem prudent to make every effort to prepare the mother physically and mentally to cope with the sensations and discomfort of birth in order to avoid the use of such medicaments" (ibid.).

WHERE DOES IT HURT?

Note in the second quote above the avoidance of the use of the term "pain". Consistently in these accounts, breathing and relaxation are regarded as proper methods to relieve stress in childbirth; pain is presented as a symptom of fear not necessarily relieved by drugs. However, a range of attitudes towards pain exists amongst various groups concerned with childbirth. The models of birth advocated by the Childbirth Education Association and similar community-based groups follow on from the pioneer writings of Dick-Read and Lamaze, and their practices centre around pain management (e.g. Humerick, 1984). Being able to "control" pain is seen to provide a good childbirthing experience and for some of these groups, therefore, analgesics and anaesthesia have a potential equal to active participation for ensuring a satisfying birth experience. In their publications, and in the texts of the verbal instructions in antenatal classes, women are taught a range of strategies to deal with pain which include massage, hot towels, breathing, relaxation, psychological techniques of dissociation (chanting, counting backwards, etc.), as well as the acceptance of the use of gas, pethidine injections and epidural anaesthesia, when necessary. In this view of birth, perceived pain and dissatisfaction are not directly correlated. Humerick (1984), for instance, argues that mastery—the perception of control—is a key factor in the birthing experience. On the other hand, there has been much stronger, unqualified support for natural births, which include criticism of the kind of psychoprophylaxis taught by the Childbirth Education Association. The centrality in labour of individual experience is underwritten in this regard by Lumley and Astbury (1980) who point out that the emphasis on pain in the prepared childbirth movement has obscured recognition of the individuality of each woman and her unique feelings and reactions. Differences in childbirth ideologies come into contrast in some popular journals. For example, an article in the *New Idea* (Nobel, 1985) counterposes the "prepared childbirth" (in which "she [the birthing woman] valiantly struggles to pace her breathing and focus her vision to dissociate herself from her body...fragmenting her consciousness and effort, she also worries about how well she is performing the techniques and coping with the ordeal") with "a labour of love" whereby a mother freely finds her own labour positions, makes sounds without inhibitions, enjoys support and caresses from her partner and chosen attendants, eats to appetite, drinks to thirst and generally responds in a way that feels natural to her (ibid.).

This emphasis on the individuality and the personalised and totalising experience of birth finds its most extreme examples in the popular and sympathetic treatments of radically alternative births, such as the interview with parents of Ebony, the "water baby", whose underwater birth—and near death—was captured by television cameras (Wiles, 1985), and the account of the water birth of Kiah Jeanes, who died soon after (Simpson, 1988). It is fair to observe, however, that proponents of alternative, "natural" birthing do not ignore pain—they re-define it (see, for example, Blackie as quoted above) on the basis of a number of assumptions, such as, for example, that pain in labour is learnt through fear and tension (as women in non-Western cultures are said to have painless births), and that parturition is in principle painless as any other normal, "natural" physiological process. Melzack (1984) has surveyed evidence for these assumptions, as well as a number of studies of labour pain, concluding that pain is an inevitable accompaniment of childbirth, though there is a striking range of individual differences in the level of pain experienced by women. This suggests the need to prepare the mother-to-be to cope, in various ways, if need be, with "the possibilities that may confront her at the time of birth" (Melzack, 1984:335).

In order to break the nexus between parturition and pain and thus also to dissociate birth and illness, pain in labour is discussed in the popular childbirth literature using a variety of synonyms for it. The term "contraction" is most usual, but there are also many other, more euphemistic, ones—some allusive, such as "intensity", "pressure" or "energy", others more specific, e.g. "waves" or "rushes". Thus the following is offered as an example to a labour attendant of a first-time mother: "See if you can become really sensitive to it (the rush) and see what it's trying to tell you to do, see what shape it wants you to take" (Gaskin, 1985:7).

NATURALLY CORRECT

In practice, the increased emphasis on birth without intervention has not led to a complete rejection of the medical model of birth. It has, however, led to a widespread popular belief in the general undesirability of anaesthetised delivery, in contrast to popular attitude and practice thirty years ago when obstetric intervention was welcomed as the end of painful birth. The ideal of the fully conscious birthing woman has, we feel, three aspects. Firstly, it is the prerequisite for the actual experience of parturition; secondly, it makes possible labour's desirable components of involvement and autonomy, as well the ecstasy which is supposed to build up in this situation. Thus Brook (1976), for example, advocating a non-technical and romantic model of natural birth, writes:

> Vital to Leboyer's birth attitude must be a woman's own attitude to her body, her baby and her birth-giving. Only with her participation, her calm, her lack of fear, her state of consciousness, will the method really work. She will not be able to massage her own child if she is slumped, half-conscious from drugs, she will not be able to help deliver the baby if she does not know how to work with contractions, and a forceps delivery to an unrelaxed or drugged mother hardly constitutes a gentle welcome to the child, however well-meaning the obstetrician may be (Brook, 1976:102).

And thirdly, the emphasis on full consciousness includes a puritanical stance which is associated with the moral overtones of the concept of the "natural". The puritanism feeds into euphemistic constructions of pain, discussed above, which are regarded as a "challenge and an opportunity" (Bergum, 1989:67) and as either an epiphenomenon of fear to be overcome by knowledge (e.g. Brook, 1976)—or a sensation to be embraced: "The life-force that is the pain in labour need not be feared. Let us understand it for what it is and accept it positively as a 'woman's finest hour'" (Robertson, 1982).

The proponents of natural birthing derive a great deal of their recruiting power from the moral overtones of their position. Radcliffe Richards has argued that "the good connotations of 'natural' are so deeply entrenched that once anything has been said to be natural there is usually no need to produce a separate argument for its being good" (Radcliffe Richards, 1982:80). The general denotation of "natural" is "without intervention, interference or influence". Factors of intervention or interference in particular activities are defined contextually, in opposition to the essentially unspecified referent of "natural". In this manner, the use of the term is given great manipulative potential which, when added to its taken-for-granted "good" connotations, renders the idea of the natural "one of the most useful means ever devised for establishing moral point" (Radcliffe Richards, 1982:80).[21] Thus women are made to feel that the "natural" way of giving birth is a better, more laudable, way. Some of our informants have clearly voiced this: "I was so proud to have a natural birth and N (husband) was so proud of me" (Joan); "I didn't feel confident about having it at home. But after I talked to friends I realised that was what I should be doing" (Rosalind).

Most women we interviewed aimed for a natural birth; but for many women this aim was tempered by the obvious, in the case of *primiparas*, unknown quality of labour, their belief in "keeping options open" because "anything might happen", and the reassurance they derived, the natural imperative notwithstanding, from a medical environment. In the words of one of our informants:

> The main reason I wanted to go into (the maternity hospital) was for a security blanket sort of thing, and we kind of talked about it and decided it would probably better for me...to be in a labour ward where there were people you know and machines everywhere and women in white dresses and doctors running around all the time,

---

21. For example: "With both birth and death we face the question of how far we are willing to go from the natural process *just to protect us from risk*" (Arms, 1975:144, our emphasis).

because this was the sort of thing, the sort of security I wanted...to know that there was everything there if anything did go wrong. I'm a very pessimistic sort of person and I really have no idea...if somebody asked me if I thought something was going to go wrong I'd say no, but I just think that because I don't know what's going to happen, I'm more kind of (pessimistic)...I think it is because I haven't been through it before, I don't know whether I am going to become hysterical, or need every drug under the sun, or whether I am going to be big and brave and fight it out through myself (Jennie).

ACHIEVING THE GOOD BIRTH

The arguments in favour of childbirth without intervention and the public representations of the ideal birth by the media have been compelling for many women. The popular literature on birth and the ante-natal classes, attended mainly by middle-class women, have reinforced these notions by de-emphasising possible complications of labour and delivery and by offering a model of birth that equates "good" and "success" to a birth of reasonable duration, drug free and without obstetric assistance or interference. A birth that in any way deviates from this ideal may be thought of as "bad" or "a failure". In fact, however, few women deliver according to this model of a perfect, natural birth, sustaining at least a torn perineum or succumbing to gas during labour and an episiotomy as a prelude to delivery. *Primiparas*, including also some of those who give birth at home (Bennett, 1986), are most likely to require medical intervention or to seek pain relief.

The fact that women are likely, actuarially speaking, to "fail" birth is important precisely because labour and delivery have, in terms of the current debate concerning them, ideological importance as the major events of reproduction. Women set up specific ideals, aspirations and expectations for themselves of their pregnancy[22] and labour, and any deviation from this typically leads to

---

22. Some of our respondents who had experienced complications during pregnancy, such as high blood pressure resulting in hospitalisation, or threatened miscarriage, felt that their bodies had failed them and that they had been cheated of their right to experience a "proper" pregnancy.

their self-assessment as "failure". Many of the women invested strongly in the notion of natural childbirth, which typically included the absence of any so-called "hygienic measures" (enema, shaving) and the avoidance of the use of drugs and physical interventions. But the majority would fail to meet these expectations: it proved much easier to "fail" birth than to "fail" pregnancy. Thus Anne recounted that "I had a lot of concern about having a Caesar, there was disappointment; J. (father) could not be there, and also I felt I was missing out on this event that was so built up in my mind—and I've let myself down", and Stella recalled:

> (The birth was) very quick but it had its complications...it was a great shock because it was so different from the way I expected it to be. I'd been to the physiotherapy classes which I thought would have prepared me and they didn't; I thought you'd sit up in bed and do your breathing exercises and that was it, I suddenly found myself writhing around in bed in the most dreadful agony, I've been looking forward to the birth—I must have been crazy.

As Bergum notes, women "who lose their own sense of control and experience pain, forceps, drugs, Caesarean birth, long and difficult labours often feel guilty that they have not managed well, or angry that they have not been well prepared. They are left unsure of themselves and their abilities" (1989:127).

Obstetric intervention resulting from complications during pregnancy and labour were subsequently incorporated in an acceptable manner by some women as they reconstructed their experience of birth. In recounting the story of their labour, women often adopted medical explanations that best described and explained the outcome, such that a potentially disappointing birth (i.e. one that did not fit with the "natural" model adopted prior to the event) was reversed in order to emphasise the logic of any intervention. A woman thus might shift ground, rejecting, on the basis of her own experience, the natural model of birth in favour of the medical model: "I wanted to have everything nice and natural—but there quickly came a point when I would have had anything for the pain...The doctor came very quickly...It (Caesarean, due to foetal distress) was such a relief" (Marie).

The natural model is clearly rejected in the following example where Frieda is given a way out of trying to comply with it by accepting medical advice to have an elective Caesarean: "It (the decision) was a relief. If there were to be problems (in labour) I would not know about them and would not suffer; I really did not look forward to prolonged labour, pain and possible laceration".

This pragmatic attitude sometimes presented us with interesting role-reversals, for example, from Vera, who had prolonged labour and, in due time, two epidurals: "The only thing I wasn't real keen on with him (the doctor)—he likes this natural type birth—not really impressed with the idea of pethidine and the block. But, if you've got to have, you've got to have it!...Once you're into the nitty-gritty, you think well, you're here and just keep going". Women consider a number of factors when choosing their mode of birth. Judy favoured natural childbirth and had always "liked the idea" of a birth centre. However, at 36, she elected to go to the labour ward for "(at my age) you can't be sure things won't go wrong; I like to feel an emergency can be taken care of straightaway".

Other women however maintained their allegiance to the ideals of natural childbirth and explained any intervention (that may have of necessity taken place) as unwarranted interference by the medical attendants. For many of these women who saw themselves as victims, and for those whose labours failed to meet their aspirations, the construction after the event of an acceptable account of their labours remained a problem. This has been recognised in the literature; Pilgrim (1984a), for instance, maintains that women who have a "negative birth experience" sustain a period of grief, anger and depression as they seek to reconcile expectation and outcome. Nicki felt that because the birth "went wrong", bonding with the infant was problematic and continued to be so fragile that she felt unable to return to work a year later. Hilary, another woman we interviewed, who at the age of 40 was delivered by Caesarean section of her first child (due to the fact that the foetus appeared small for date, that she was Rh-ve and that she had a suspected uterine infection), was extremely bitter of the denial to her of a "proper birth" and felt resentful towards both the obstetrician and the anaesthetist; she again maintained that bonding with her daughter had been rendered difficult as the direct result of the manner of delivery. In line with this, Bergum argues that birth is "relational", a "community activity", and that Caesarean delivery strips women of a critical point in terms of bonding: the "embodied experience of 'giving' birth enables women to learn to take responsibility for the child which may be missed in Caesarean deliveries" (Bergum, 1989:92).

Ideas like these are widespread; as we have already shown, criticisms of interventions in childbirth—including, perhaps particularly, Caesarean deliveries—have been quite common in the popular literature for some time. It may therefore be difficult to separate the effects of such information on women's perceptions of birth and subsequent experiences, from the effects on them of the actual events involved in the birth.

A few women in the study were particularly rigid in their notions of what constituted "proper" pregnancy and birth and in what they desired for themselves, and accordingly they were badly shaken by unanticipated variation. Sandra, for example, was thrown by the prematurity of delivery and her precipitous labour, although not by the medical intervention *per se*:

> I missed out on the last month of pregnancy, the real anticipatory month. I missed out on that, I missed out on all the tiredness and feeling heavy and feeling frumpy, and for me that was part of the pregnancy as well...to suddenly get (the baby) one month early, that was all wrong, that didn't seem right, that wasn't part of the plan, you know...and then to have a really quick labour, and all that went with that...I want him now back inside me, I want that build up next time.

Sandra's disappointment relates to the experiences of other women whose labours also deviated from the ideal they had anticipated, especially with respect to the degree of satisfaction with the psychological experience of the event. This disappointment was very often compounded with guilt and anxiety felt by those women who thought that by allowing intervention and seeking pain relief, they had "weakened" and "succumbed" to assistance: "I was rattled, it (the epidural) would not have happened otherwise...I still regret it" (Fran).

In the examples discussed so far we encounter a paradoxical trend in the evolution of cultural attitudes to birth. The possibility of pleasure in the birth experience, originally based on the confidence in the soundness of medical procedures and the comparative freedom from pain ensured by them, has evolved into a cultural ideal where this pleasure is now both a requirement for, and a criterion of, a completely unadulterated, spontaneous, "natural" (i.e. not "medicalised") birth. This standard is experienced by many women as an anxiety-provoking constraint. The current prescriptions for the ideal "good birth" experience, being quite puritanical in their judgemental connotations, have thus become a negation, in fact, of the ease and comfort—and possibly pleasure—that might have been reasonably expected from the developments in labour management during the 1920s–1930s.

Of course this proposition relates to general trends and is an abstraction based on a number of sources. In practice, it is not necessarily equally applicable to each of them. As already stated, many women are prepared to be quite eclectic in their attitudes and practices in relation to birth; and public discourse also is, at some levels, very pleasingly situated in a context of moderation and commonsense (e.g. Magney, 1987). Consistent with our data, Michaelson and Alvin (1988) also note an eclecticism that has characterised American births in recent times; in their study, although all women took Lamaze or natural birth classes, they expected to have conservatively managed births, expected to have some anaesthesia and were by and large not disappointed with it when it was given. Similarly, at least one woman wanted a Caesarean birth to avoid the pain of labour[23]: "This attitude towards childbirth reinforced the tendency of many physicians to admit technological interventions in the birth process. In addition, the high rate of intervention, particularly electronic fetal

---

23. Like Frieda from our study, mentioned earlier in this chapter.

monitoring and anaesthesia, reinforced most women's views that this was the 'right way to have a baby'" (Michaelson and Alvin, 1988:148).

SUBJECTS TO FAILURE

The eclectic tendencies notwithstanding, the *"praxis"* of everyday life is embedded in ideologies. The tension between the opposing medical and natural models is at issue primarily when an individual is situated so that alternative ways of seeing become a major concern. A woman who accepts a natural model of birth is almost always confronted subsequently with a conflict of ideology, since, not surprisingly, few medical practitioners reject the medical model of pregnancy and birth. Women are often aware, implicitly at least, of the ideological conflict that underpins the doctor-patient relationship, and seek to negotiate with their practitioner the grounds for obstetric intervention at the time of labour and delivery, gaining reassurance that intervention will not occur as a matter of routine. Negotiation then may recur during the pregnancy in the face of unanticipated complications (e.g. breech presentation) as well as during labour and at the time of delivery. The reassurance of the practitioner can be, and often is, formulaic—he or she would intervene only if there were medical indications—but of course the identification of such indications remains in medical hands. Women strongly committed to a "natural" birth frequently anticipate labour as a battle of wills, yielding ground as they lose a sense of authority and control once they are on medical territory, i.e. at the hospital. The subsequent assessment of birth as "failed", where intervention has occurred or where the labouring woman has resorted to drugs, is the consequence of the perceived defeat of a natural paradigm by a medical one.

Conflict is minimised at home births and intervention, when it occurs, does not constitute the defeat of a belief system. This in part relates to the trust established between the woman and her attendants, both because they are guests (and employees) on her territory (in the case of home births), and because they have relinquished their strict adherence to a medical model of birth in any case, so that the woman can retain a sense of personal authority, power and control. At a home birth and, to an extent, at a birth-centre, medicine becomes a technical back-up to an experience that is woman-centred and woman-controlled, in contrast to a hospital birth wherein the labouring woman becomes the subject of obstetric practice. Homebirth doctors and midwives (and staff at birth-centres) have accepted the validity of criticisms of hospital-based obstetrics and share the general ideological stance of the parturient woman and her lay helpers. Given the absence of ideological conflict, intervention when it does occur is reported in quite a different light. For example, a published report of a home birth in a partisan magazine (Anon, 1982) presented technical intervention thus:

> By 1.30 p.m., after no progress for 4 hours, Peter (the attending practitioner) wanted to break the waters. Had I been in hospital, I probably would have over-reacted and refused this interference, but because I knew Peter would not take such measures purely for experience, I was happy for him to do what was considered necessary.

Another birth report in a similar publication (Taylor, 1982) offers an even more dramatic accommodation of obstetric intervention without challenging natural birthing ideology. It is worth quoting the setting of the birth firstly, to bring this into sharp relief. The mother writes:

> As events so often happen for us, just at the last moment, just before you think it's all a bit too much—our 'house' happened. Perched on a rock completely enveloped by eucalyptus and marvellous natural bush, overlooking a deep tree-filled valley—a tiny hexagonal dwelling with huge windows in each direction, no doors, wood stove, and hessian-lined walls...we revelled in the vital energy of the place...we looked forward for the first time with a deep joy to our home birth.

In candlelight, to background music, a son, Sky, was born: "Maggie (the midwife) gently and patiently massaged the area (perineum) for maximum elasticity. I still couldn't push him out so, opting for a small episiotomy, *which I didn't feel*, and with great effort, the baby's head made it through....the rest of his little body slid out quickly" (our emphasis). Such accounts of natural childbirth in its partisan literature are generally given in glowing terms; for example "a process so awe-inspiring that it is difficult to describe without becoming intensely poetic or religious" (Arms, 1975:181).

We have argued that anxiety concerning "success" at giving birth is a dominant theme of the contemporary woman's experience of labour. This anxiety is the result of the ideological construction of birth which in the 80s has centred on the actions and sensations of the mother and which is at variance with—and often positively antagonistic to—older models of labour management that still dominate professional obstetric practice. Amidst the reverberations from this clash, women have had a hard time indeed. To prove that birth is natural, hence to prove the validity of the model of birth to which they adhere, or, at least, to meet the expectations that are self-imposed upon adopting this ideal, the labouring woman must, in a hospital setting, avoid any complication or deviation in labour, or any concessions to, or acceptance of, technical-medical assistance. While the ultimate "failure" is a Caesarean delivery followed by lactation failure, any variation may be read as the invalidation of a belief system by the parturient woman, and as grounds for imputed triumph of the medical establishment and the technological imperative. A torn perineum "proves" the value of routine episiotomy in medical eyes, for instance, and so demonstrates the woman's inability to perfect delivery. The consequent stitch provides material evidence of the indispensability of obstetric supervision and control—and therefore, of the weakness of self and of the fallacy of the belief in a natural birth.

Such constructed failures may be negated subsequently. A newspaper article, for instance, recounts the experiences of a woman giving birth to her second child one year after the Caesarean birth of her first. Despite a little shave, enema, induction with syntocyn, gas, gas again, an epidural, a top-up and finally stirrups and ventouse to deliver the baby, the woman comments: "I heard my doctor tell David he could have got the baby out much earlier if he had done an episiotomy. I'm very grateful to him. I am so happy I did it myself without having to have a cut... *Having a natural birth makes you feel more of a woman*" (Gemmell-Smith, 1986, our emphasis).

Loss of control, weakness and failure are made explicit in may of the texts of natural birth. In one early such work, Erna Wright comments:

> A trained woman cannot "fail". There is nothing in which to fail. She knows all she needs to do is handle her sensations exactly as she has been taught; then she can remain in control; of course her husband and the team who are with her during her labour may need to help her to reinforce her control...terms like "success" or "failure" are meaningless. Women don't go into labour as an endurance test or an obstacle-race. But they can go into labour armed with a valuable means of remaining on top of their own experience...therefore any woman with commonsense can be trained so that she herself becomes a most useful and co-operative member of the obstetric team which watches over her own, and her baby's well-being, before and birth...learning how to birth is like any other skill—learning to ride a bicycle, drive a car, play a musical instrument...or indeed learning to read or write for that matter (Wright, 1974:18-20).

Here, despite reassurances to the contrary, notions of failure are central to the model. The labouring woman, the quintessential Weberian worker, child of Protestant capitalism, fails through lack of effort, commitment and learnt skill; indeed, Wright continues (1974:23-240), women must "work harder" to remember their lessons in order to overcome the biological handicaps of "maternal amnesia".

BIRTH MEANINGS AND METAPHORS

So labour and delivery are a battle-ground not only between two opposing sets of cultural norms concerning childbirth (Lumley and Astbury, 1980), but also between medical practitioners and patients where they do not share common ideals and principles. However, as some of the examples above have shown, even where the natural model is fully accepted, the possibility of anxiety over "failure" still remains and the grounds for it have to be rationalised away. A more genuinely liberal, accepting and reasonable attitude is required to support women in the practicalities of choosing and seeing through—or adapting—their options with regard to labour and delivery. The very availability of these options is in accord with current emphases on choices in life-styles and self-projections (Lasch, 1985). This may be seen as being liberating, even if we take into account the sociological axiom that no choices are totally "free". But while the availability of choice represents a current cultural value, the anxiety over the success within the chosen option is compounded by the tension inherent in the clash of the belief-systems that provide these choices (Crouch and Manderson, 1987a). Perhaps this is because women feel that these choices are solicited, as well as made available, by parties in a conflict of interests the grounds for which go beyond disagreements about birth procedures and their consequences for women.

Pregnancy, birth and early mothering provide a site for the enactment of tensions that are evident in society at large. An analysis of the social process of reproduction and the cultural representations of motherhood reflect and allow for an elaboration of these tensions between professional and lay. However, the professional/lay conflicts over the control of reproduction are themselves largely the product of other tensions. One is that of male/female, as reflected most succinctly and commonly in the male obstetrician/female patient contrast. Another is technical/natural, wherein the medical profession, its institutional base and the medical paradigm of birth, all representing elaborations of "the technical", are opposed to the reproductive woman in the domestic, private, sphere, allied with the natural model within the sphere of "the natural". The unfolding of these tensions is a historical process that has been under way for some time, becoming visible, as we have already suggested, during the last decade. As

Richman and Goldthorp (1978) point out, birth is a theme that has become politically fused at all levels.

The cultural expression of these tensions assumes a number of symbolic forms. The language of medicine, when dealing with infection and disease, is the language of metaphor, most frequently the metaphor of war (Sontag, 1978). Battles are fought, campaigns mounted, strategies planned against invasive organisms and colonising malignant cells, fights are won or lost, the disease is either arrested or conquered or the patient succumbs. Birth—structurally in opposition to death—is portrayed within a different metaphoric frame, albeit one that is common also to depictions of real battles and warfare. This is the metaphor of the theatre: of drama, actors, scripts, orchestra and stage. And as battles, of opposing armies and people against diseases, are planned, so too the performance of birth is planned: roles are allocated, scripts for the ideal birth are written, the stage is set and the drama anticipated, enacted and recounted.

Oakley's prose, serving to introduce the accounts of British women of their pregnancies and births, is exemplary of the use of imagery from the performing arts to sustain her narrative. Scenarios of tests, interviews and examinations unfold; spotlights fall on the doctor and the pregnant woman; their encounters are scripted (1986a:44). Birth for the expectant mother is an "approaching drama" that includes "scenes of horror and disaster" as well as of joy (p.83). Birth itself is "one of the most important dramas of a woman's life" (p.112); its scenes are relived and reworked to explain the points of deviation from the pre-scripted birth, the birthplan of prepared childbirth (p.111). New motherhood continues the play: "the social role of mother is only rehearsed, the stage is set...but motherhood is unreal when it is acted out in an institution" (p.140). In some cases, Oakley writes, transition to motherhood is aided by the mother's mother: she "acts as scriptwriter, director, stage-manager and producer all in one" (p.148).

Metaphors from film-making also prevail: birth is, according to Oakley, a film in the pregnant woman's "mind's eye" (p.80) and the presence and involvement of partners at birth evoke ideas of viewing—"it was like seeing a good film"—and of action: "once drama takes over, the role sits more comfortably on their (men's) shoulders, and they become necessary (and usually grateful) actors" (p.206-7). As already noted more than a decade ago (Richman and Goldthorp, 1978), men have become important actors in the drama of birth, increasingly so in recent years: "Fathers-to-be have come a long way in the past few years: from extra to bit-part actor to co-star, even birth-manager and onto nursing father" (*Parents and Children Magazine*, 1986:2). Within the process of teasing out the cultural practices of childbearing and in the context of the metaphors of performance employed in this part of the discussion, it is now most appropriate to give some attention to the role of the father in the cultural script of birth.

THE ADVENT OF MEN

Male presence at birth is by no means new; like other aspects of the movement to lessen the influence of the medical model over birth, it has considerable history. While most women laboured and delivered alone amongst hospital staff in the 1950s and 1960s, there is evidence of consumer interest in, if not pressure for, the presence of fathers at birth from the early 60s on. For example, the *Australian Women's Weekly* (1 March 1961) gives an extraordinary vision of a painless labour that would allow, in the hour before delivery: "those dear familiar husband's hands caressing our hair, to chat quietly about the little everyday things which mean so much, to have him wipe our hands when they become clammy— to share the anticipation and halve the apprehension" (Rae, 1961:47).

An early text on natural birth provides the ideological basis for the involvement of men at birth, in the role of "a sort of plumber's mate to your wife during this job she has to do" (Wright, 1974:200). The father's presence is important for the child as well: "You are assisting your wife to give it the best possible start in life" (Wright, 1974:201). In addition, birth as family affair may circumvent the Freudian hazards of parenting: "no woman whose husband has been willing and privileged to share this experience with her will ever become possessive about this child" (Wright, 1974:203).

Nevertheless, it is only in recent years that there has been general discussion of, and advocation for, male participation in labour that has resisted and finally dissolved the "cultural conspiracy against fatherhood in modern times" (Richman and Goldthorp, 1978:157). "Birth as a joint activity (of both parents)" (Richman, 1982), as discussed in sociological literature in the 1980s and popular literature on birth and early motherhood, suggests that "we are in the midst of a huge "joy of fatherhood" cultural media blitz" (Dix, 1986). In this literature, there is a marked linguistic and ideological shift: from the mother herself to the total situation that allowed the presence of middle class men at birth (cf. Michaelson, 1988a:7). It is indeed easy to see the link between the presence of fathers at birth and the drive to domesticate labour and naturalise delivery. Less evident, perhaps, is the possibility that the father, as an unquestionably significant male presence, is meant to share with and therefore take away from the indispensability and importance of the hitherto sovereign figure, now the other man in the proceedings, the (usually) male obstetrician—and even, maybe, to deflect from him the orgasmic waves of the now recognisably sexual experience of labour.

For some women in our sample, the involvement of their male partners at birth was a means of incorporating them, of smoothing over an exclusion with which they felt uncomfortable; this was linked to their notion of reproduction as an act of a couple rather than of an individual. Thus Sally wrote in her pregnancy diary: "Man seemed to be allowed absolutely no place in the scheme of things...I feel indignant for (men, that they) are excluded by women from any part of the birth process. Sure, men now watch birth but thereafter it seems more the case that women reject paternity for being akin to maternity".

Sandra's argument for her husband's presence at birth picked up these same sentiments, a concern at the female dominance of birth: "I feel really sorry for men, they can't feel it (the *in utero* infant) and don't know. They are definitely second class, well in the background, when it comes to having a baby".

On the other hand, Margaret's reasons for her partner's presence at birth included his "natural" right to witness the birth of his child, an obligation on him to provide her with support and to witness the discomfort of childbirth and, as well, to be there at the critical time for his future relationship with the newborn:

> I'd always said I wouldn't do it (birth) alone and it's his child so he has every right to be there and to witness the pain…It'll be an emotional time for us, binding the two of us together, and bonding us three: they keep talking about birth and bonding between the baby and the mother, and never about the father. But it must be as important, as crucial, and it's got to be done at the same time if possible—it can't hurt the baby.

Other women echo these sentiments: "Oh, I wouldn't like him not to be there. I'd much rather him be there. It's ours, it's something we're doing together" (Anne), and "I just think, well, if you've conceived this kid together, they jolly well should be there to see what we go through" (Linda).

There is also some evidence in women's accounts that attendants at birth, including husbands, sometimes take on responsibility of ensuring that the woman maintains control and does not "give in". For example:

> I'd lost control y'know, that's what disappointed me most…like you know when it was actually born I wanted it to be very easy so that it did not tear me, and I did not have to be cut. I lost control and I couldn't, didn't know what was going on. And ah, I lost control of my breathing and everything. Graeme was standing there all the time saying breathe, breathe, breathe, breathe! Keep breathing! But then I'd sort of go for the gas and he'd say no, don't have the gas—breathe! And I would go I want it, I want it, I want it! He'd say you can do it, you can do it!…I think I threw myself around quite a bit…the next day…my face was sore, down there where I put the mask on, from holding it on (Helen).

The popular literature emphasises these and other sentiments, highlighting particularly the strengthening of the relationship between the partners through the mutual experience of birth. This is described as "something incomparably beautiful, moving and important", the "dramatic hours of labour and birth" being also "an experience which binds many couples even more closely together" (*Parents and Children Magazine*, 1986:51). Published personal accounts reflect this theme. For example, a father writes:

> Only once or twice did I feel that we were losing control (the contractions becoming too much for my wife), but hard concentration on level D (counting out aloud together) soon rescued the situation... (The hospital staff) made us feel that it was our experience to share together (Anon, 1984a:29).

Another example of a father's report:

> Our birth was a wonderful experience. I was full of love and admiration for Robyn. She had done so well. It was her birth, but she'd allowed me such a close and sharing role in it...We'd been planning and rehearsing parts of our birth for months. Videos, classes, meetings seemed to go on endlessly. It was a relief to be on the other side (Allan, 1985:32–3).

The emphasis on the sharing of the experience for the couple recurs in women's reports: "My husband was a fantastic help to me and guided my breathing and pushing. He really enjoyed the labour. He was very good in the first stage, telling me not to be negative and to go with it and breathe" (Anon, 1984b). And according to one of the women we interviewed, "If I hadn't had my husband there I'd never have...it would have been dreadful. I often think about my mum, you know (she) had four children, and the husbands were not allowed anywhere near them. 'Cause you just need that support, 'cause it's such a long day. Just so slow" (Denise).

These last contributions make it clear that the father may participate, as well as assist, in labour but cannot share the parturition. Indeed, the assisting function has been recognised by the medical profession years before the father's own experience of birth became generally accepted as an important component of the event. Work by Henneborn and Cogan (1975), for example, suggests that the husband's presence in labour was important in affecting reported pain (by the mother); partners' presence tends to correlate with reduced use of medication and provides other practical support to labouring women supplementing the work of the obstetrical team (see Block and Block, 1975; Bennett *et al.*, 1985). Recently the assistance to the mother (rather than to the attending obstetricians) has received greater attention, paralleling the shift in emphasis generally from the activities of the professionals to the actions and feelings of the woman in labour. However, in addition, there is now also an emphasis on the specific nature of the father's feelings about pregnancy and birth and on his own part in the drama of birth, a part which has now gone beyond the role of a supporting—albeit best—actor.

POST-PATRIARCHY FATHERS IN LABOUR

In this book we consider pregnancy, birth and early motherhood mainly from the point of view of women, and therefore consider the situation of men mainly through women's eyes and in relation to their experiences. Although in our research we did not interview men, much has been gleaned about their situation from our interviews and images projected in the printed media. Mid-decade, a comprehensive special section on fathers in a popular periodical (*Parents and Children Magazine*, 1986) discusses the "difficult task of becoming a man" because "a lot is expected of a man once it is certain a baby is on the way" (p.48). Though it is recognised that the man is marginal in this situation, advice on practical steps is offered to reduce this marginality: attendance at any ultrasound, joint visitation to the maternity hospital or birth centre, introduction to the obstetrician and/or midwife in advance, choice of hospital to allow presence at delivery including Caesarean section should this eventuate, and so on.

Birth itself is presented as "hours which no man can forget", an experience marked however by the ambiguity of the emotion that it generates: discomfort, unhappiness, exhilaration, joy, sexual anxiety ("many fathers no longer consider the vagina as a purely sexual organ...they now sense the enormous power that can emanate from it"). In addition, the difficulty that men experience in being at the birth as the support person, rather than in taking centre stage, is stressed, as is the range of possible behaviours that might be required of them at the moment—from passive generalised support to the hard work of constant massage, for example: "My hand was already numb after half an hour but I could not take even a second's break. At some stage I lost all sense of time. I was very exhausted after the birth but I felt I had made my contribution" (ibid:49).

Finally the article stresses men's experiences of the pain, the reality of true *couvade*, of how the men suffer, of how in the men's accounts of their experiences "the contractions had seemed endless and how they had 'pushed' too when the time came" (ibid:51).

Men's descriptions of their witnessing of and participation in the birth of their children echo these themes: "I was more on edge and excited than I have ever been...I reckon I worked almost as hard as Gail to have that baby. I did all the breathing with her and when he was finally born, I was really exhausted" (*The Australian Women's Weekly*, July 1986:150), and "I found it one of the greatest experiences of my life...it wasn't hard to share in the pain my wife experienced" (Kerstake, 1985:8).

Thus the currently emerging popular discourse on the role of fathers suggests that the earlier role of men as supporters of labouring women has slipped to one that is analogous to other types of *couvade*. We may, following Paige and Paige (1981), look for explanations of *couvade* in psychoanalytic terms, as a ritual expression of a number of unconscious fears and desires; or, following Bettelheim (1962), see it in broader terms as reflecting men's unconscious desire to actualise the feminine aspects of their (bisexual) nature. At the same time this shift in emphasis may operate to downplay the role of women in reproduction: that men can do it too at birth provides a social response to women at (paid) work. The available data from and about Australian men can fit with any of these interpretations of the competition between men and women that is now enacted at birth as on other stages; this includes men's right to be involved in decision-making regarding terminations.

The notion of the pregnant father, the incorporation of men into childbirth education classes and the emphasis on the singularity of the experience of birth that has been expanded to incorporate men as well as women, give men status where previously only women have occupied an important position. The rituals of pregnancy and birth dramatise parenthood and convert adults into parents. These rituals are performed for a community of observers (Paige and Paige, 1981) consisting not only of those witness to the birth, but also the continuing audience of others, friends and kin, to whom the story of the birth is retold, wherein the father of the infant is accorded a certain place. His involvement, activities and responses become as integral a part of the birth story as the processes of labour and the mother's own experience.

As suggested above, it may be the case that the presence of men at birth, and particularly their witnessed participation in women's rites, is a response to the increased economic and personal autonomy of women (as has also been observed in small-scale societies by Paige and Paige [1981]). However, over and above this competition—and partly because of it—there is also the reality of the decline in the stability of modern marriages and established heterosexual relationships generally. This brings to mind the seemingly puzzling contradiction in the comparison of the traditional role of fathers in birth—i.e. absence—with their current significant part in birthing: on the one hand, men are making their appearance on the scene at the very time when their position in the family (as well as the need, in some cases, for their presence in the structure) are questioned, yet, on the other hand, they were kept away from birth when there were no doubts about, or challenges to, their position.

Perhaps this contradiction is at least partly resolved if we view the presence of fathers at birth as a symbolic affirmation of the couple's relationship in a social context where the blue-print for such relationships has become blurred. In the past, fathers were absent from birth precisely because their status—together with its role implications—was unquestioned, whereas now their participation in the rituals of birth is a response to the uncertainty concerning men's roles and the multiplicity of values and expectations in relation to them. The hoped-for instantaneous "bonding" at birth is not only for the infant's benefit; the parents themselves need to partake of its magic in order to secure their future as a couple within the family that cannot, as a matter of course, be expected to hold them together in the long run.

It is possible to consider this situation from yet another perspective, at the level of objectified public images. Childbirth has been a central experience of women's lives, the singular event that gives them difference from men. Since childbirth is the means by which social adulthood is conferred on women, celibate, barren and otherwise non-reproductive women remain potentially marginal because of their failure to reproduce, whether for social or for physiological reasons. Even though there may be a devaluation of activities related to motherhood and mothering in certain contexts, pregnancy and birth still have considerable cultural prestige which each woman recognises as she moves from a childless to the with-child state. Birth has been the one domain that is exclusively female, the territory where women are at the centre and with power—however often that power has been channelled, in various ways, by others attending to her when in labour.

Futuristic technological innovation forecasts, such as male pregnancy using the abdomen as womb, challenge the sex exclusivity of birth. The involvement of men at birth foreshadows this: we have seen that over time, male presence has been given increasing status and emphasis.[24] The attrition of parturition as a female event and a woman-centred activity and its redefinition as

---

24. Block and colleagues (1981) argue that this is important in light of a perceived gatekeeper role of husbands.

part of a couple's or family history, have begun to redistribute the prestige and power of birth and its natural integrity and female sovereignty—which is now in any case threatened by the new (man-made) reproductive technologies.[25]

Our interpretations of the significance of fathers' presence at birth are not put forward as alternatives to one another, but rather as components of a very complex picture. The inconsistency which this picture projects is a common feature of symbolic manifestations, free as these can be from rational constraints.

CONTRADICTORY DEVELOPMENTS

The blurring of the borders previously delineating birth as exclusively female territory (lived in, though not necessarily ruled by, women) takes place within a set of circumstances which presents women with deep contradictions. Where women have little autonomy and power in the birthing process, and where they are treated as objects of medical procedures which emphasise the physical aspects of labour, the procedures nevertheless focus on *them* and their bodies (albeit as "precious vessels")—and thus render them centrally important. Conversely, where emphasis is placed on women's experience of birth and their autonomy and control within the process, more attention is in fact given to the *setting* in which labour takes place—and thus the "significant others", who constitute an important part of that setting, come to share personal importance with the mother.

---

25. The literature on reproductive technology is now extensive. A majority is concerned with the way in which women have been subject to biotechnological control as a result of these procedures; women's participation in programs such as those concerned with IVF is seen to reflect the power of an ideology that continues to value women firstly in terms of their reproductive ability. The current concerns continue to centre on IVF procedures, but also on ethical, legal, political and social aspects of surrogacy; a few researchers also have given some attention to other technical procedures such as prenatal diagnosis. Among recent publications, see, for example, Corea (1987), Oakley (1987), Scutt (1988), Rothman (1989), McNeil, Varcoe and Yearley (1990), Woliver (1991) and the special issue of *Women's Health Issues* (1991).

These contradictions extend as we observe that there is a sense in which, for women, negotiated choices of certain procedures in an obstetrically managed labour are factual acts of control over the process (of which an elective Caesarean for reasons of pain avoidance is perhaps the clearest and most extreme example, however paradoxically such a decision results in total submission of the woman to medical procedures). On the other hand, the control and autonomy claimed for women in the natural model of birth contain their own paradoxes, since in this model women actually relinquish conscious regulatory intentions to the "natural" biological process of labour. In this context, women are "in charge" to the extent to which they can control their reactions to the natural processes of labour. They do not, however, control the process itself and their "autonomy" in relation to it consists of their reliance on psychological and emotional support from "significant others", rather than on medical aids, for relief from the distress of labour and for help with parturition which women, after all, can rarely manage entirely on their own. During birth, there can be no true autonomy, since potentially critical physiological elements are inherent in its nature (Crouch and Manderson, 1993).

Practices relating to labour and images of birth, expressive as they are of significant cultural themes, are central to the process of embedding motherhood in the dynamic of social life. For this reason chronology has not governed the sequencing of our chapters in this section and pregnancy will be considered following, rather than preceding, the discussion of birth. In our culture, pregnancy derives its significance from birth, the event in which it culminates and towards the perfection of which the pregnant women—but now also pregnant couples—assiduously labour, in the contemporary scene of antenatal training that is as symbol-rich as it is busy. It is to this scene, with its own contradictions and paradoxes, that our attention turns in the following chapter.

PART THREE
BEFORE AND AFTER
THE EVENT

Chapter 4

BELABOURING THE PREGNANT BODY

In teasing out the cultural processes of childbearing and child-birth, we have examined the roles allocated to and assumed by each actor. In this view of childbirth as performance, the hours of labour and delivery are the play: a one-off, largely improvised performance of indeterminate duration and no previously fixed starting time. The relative unpredictability of the event notwith-standing, the actors—the birthing mother and her attendants—anticipate the plot development according to an already written script that sets out the general guidelines and provides the basis for rehearsals and the arrangement of props.

Pregnancy offers various occasions for rehearsals, although significantly these are practised primarily by those largely middle-class couples who attend ante-natal classes. Here alterna-tive scenarios are carefully sketched out and actors' roles are modelled to fit possible developments, so that during the actual performance, improvisation along the main theme lines is possible. Thus "lines" are learned—breathing, rhythmic panting, massage and verbal techniques to detract from pain, for example. All these "lines" can also be rehearsed at home.

During this formal rehearsal period, each "pregnant couple", as class instructors tend to call the pregnant mother and her partner, can select elements for their own personalised script from a wide range of possible production directions for each stage of labour and delivery: Shave? Yes or no, perineal or extended, done at home or in hospital, by self, partner, midwife or nurse? Or, active or passive labour: lie, walk, stand, squat? Perineal massage, if so, by whom, at what stage (continued during crowning or not)? Mirror at the time of crowning? Ditto for photographs? Who is first to "discover" the sex of the baby[26]: partner, the mother herself, the midwife? The list of options is, in fact, phenomenally long, covering not only actions and words, but also props: cameras, film, favourite pictures/posters to domesticate the birthplace, glucose tablets, barley sugar, hot soup, massage oil, lanolin, lipchap, bean bag, mirror, hand-fan, pen, paper, games to play and/or books (in case of a slow labour), radio or special taped music, thick sox, and so on.[27]

Yet the choices that really matter are limited and define and constrain the experience of birth. The availability of such choices is a relative one; both hospitals and obstetricians vary greatly with respect to optional procedures which they offer and publicise, and women must often select their obstetrician or other birth attendants, and the venue for birth, in the context of certain limitations: there are only a few birth centres for example, and often hospitals have strict rules about which women may deliver in them, first choice of obstetrician may not be possible, and so on. Even so, the image of choice and the pervasive ideas which form this image influence the way in which reproduction is understood and mould social expectations and assessments of birth. At the individual's

---

26. Since the 1980s, the sex of the baby is known before birth for an increasing number of parents as the result of relatively commonplace antenatal tests.

27. Homebirths require even more props. One birth report includes the following: "With about four weeks to go, (we) were still thinking about helpers and making lists of things to buy and things to do. It included the following: fast film, blue filter, batteries for torch, plastic sheet, apricot kernel oil, flyswat, rescue remedies, shoelace (for the emergency birth), chop wood, borrow extra heater, extra candles, pack bag ready for hospital, pack baby things in alfoil, fill freezer full of food, pick up sterile bundle, move furniture around, contact acupuncturist, etc." (Allan, 1985:30).

level, these expectations are generally developed during pregnancy.

As we have already pointed out, pregnancy is experienced as a
process rather than a state of being. In its course, women and their
partners gather information about and train for birth, practising a
variety of skills and methods that are designed to limit the discomfort and maximise the facility with which a child is born, and to
enhance the pleasure of the experience. The pamphlets, magazine
and newspaper articles, books and other publications on the
subject of pregnancy and birth that have appeared in abundance
during the last decade or so, provide the basic information that is
supplemented for many by activities such as ante-natal physiotherapy classes, childbirth education classes and hospital tours.
The majority of publications are sympathetic to the natural childbirth movement and incorporate a critique, implicit or explicit, of
an obstetrician-controlled, medicalised birth and delivery. The
births that are advocated within the literature are ones with
minimum intervention in mind.

IMAGES OF OBSTETRICS

In practice most women are monitored throughout their pregnancies by obstetricians and delivered by them in hospital labour
wards, with the consequence of the potential of conflict between
reality and expectations and often also between women and their
attendants. In this connection we may note the discrepancy in attitudes to birth and pregnancy, in so far as technical procedures
such as chorionic villus biopsy, amniocentesis and ultrasound
during pregnancy are regarded as desirable and valuable while
most interventions during labour and delivery are seen as invasive.

Critics of obstetric and gynecological practice in relation to
pregnancy have highlighted the objectification of women: the
reduction of the subject woman to body parts, in this case, the
uterus (Oakley, 1986b). Criticisms from women of ante-natal
examinations centre on this objectification and depersonalisation,
as well as the impersonal and ritual nature of the activities of

monitoring: weighing, urine testing, the taking of blood-pressure, the external physical examination to detect the height of the fundus and, late in pregnancy, the position of the foetus. These activities may take only minutes, some being carried out by a nurse or receptionist rather than the medical practitioner; it is atypical for the examination to contain other, more personal, elements. Doctor-patient interaction is therefore limited and circumscribed. The question "How are you?" is a routine one that does not invite from the pregnant woman more than a routine response; minimal interaction discourages the questioning of doctor by patient. Pregnant women are counselled in popular books on pregnancy and by lay educators (e.g. ante-natal class instructors) to make a list of questions to ask their doctor—not because of any forgetfulness attributed to pregnancy, but because of the short time routinely allocated to ante-natal examination and the impersonality that usually characterises the doctor-patient relationship and discourages the exchange of ideas on the management of labour and delivery.

Since the obstetrician is generally a man, the maintenance of his impersonal attitude towards the woman and the reduction of the woman to the status of pregnant uterus desexualise the doctor-patient relationship—perhaps not altogether an unnecessary measure from his point of view, at least. We have found that many women show affection and proprietary feelings towards their obstetricians despite the studied detachment of the latter; some even symbolically name their sons after them. It is quite possible that the feminist critique of obstetric practice has, in any case, exaggerated the detachment of the obstetricians from their patients, projecting into this critique, on the one hand, its value-judgments of men in general and professional men in particular—and on the other, women's subconscious frustration with the clinical treatment of a condition which for them is socially, emotionally and sexually overdetermined. It is not surprising, then, that ecstatic accounts of birth in contemporary iconic descriptions of it coincide with the renaissance of the midwife as the (sometimes) chief attendant and the idealisation of un-doctored birth; and, the metaphor of orgasm having been established, that fathers have become important participants in the process of pregnancy and birth—ensuring that the now openly acknowledged libidinal charge is confronted by its rightful object.

The obstetricians described by the women in our study do not correspond fully to the stereotypes presented in the critical accounts of the profession. They are often, though not of course always, described as quite human and have been variously characterised as considerate, understanding and willing to answer questions and negotiate issues. In our study, observations regarding objectification and depersonalisation, excess of clinical zeal and lack of human concern, are based rather more on the system as a whole and on the tenor of the routine procedures, including administrative ones, to which women are subjected during pregnancy and birth.

We can see that the disembodiment of the uterus from its context as a consequence of the singularity of medical vision and concerns is perhaps the most marked in diagnostic procedures of pregnancy, such as in ultrasound and blood tests, and particularly amniocentesis and chorionic villus sampling. These are times when the medical technique is being performed to check the health and viability of the conception. Such occasions are emotionally complex for the pregnant woman; for example as a result of the first, almost always thrilling, sight of the foetus, fear of abnormality can be brought to the surface, or there may be anxiety concerning risk of loss of foetus as the consequence of the procedure. Typically little or no counselling is provided and little encouragement is given to the woman to seek support from her obstetrician either prior to, at the time of, or after the tests while she awaits the results. The tests themselves are, not surprisingly, conducted in highly mechanical fashion. Foetal safety is allied to the technical competence of the geneticist who is concerned firstly and foremostly with the procedure (Rapp, 1988b; Rothman, 1988), and although there is considerable variation among individuals, there is usually limited exchange between patient and geneticist. As a rule, they do not meet until the time of the procedure and follow-up is through the woman's own obstetrician or general practitioner. The woman's body here is clearly the object of medical interest rather than the subject of personal professional concern.

THE ALTERNATIVE VIEW

While obstetric focus is fixed on the uterus and the *in utero* foetus, in practices that flow from alternative models other parts of the body are also given meaning and treated as if pregnant. On inspection, these practices are no more holistic than those of medicine despite ideological utterances along these lines. The pregnant/ labouring body remains a composite of parts; the difference is that the parts of the body related to reproduction are extended in these alternative models.

Ante-natal exercise classes provide us with an illustration of this extended mechanical vision of the body. Since the uterus is a muscle over which the labouring woman has very little, if any, control, it is on other muscles that the classes focus. The exercise regime taught to women in these classes and outlined in pamphlets, magazine liftouts and books identifies specific groups of muscles and ligaments and distinct functions and/or phases associated with them. Despite variations that depend on the instructor and the specific philosophy that guides particular exercise regimens, generally some nine distinct groups of exercises that are taught. These are those designed to prevent or alleviate discomforts of pregnancy, e.g. backache, leg-cramps, bladder incontinence (pelvic floor inadequacy); those designed to influence the outcome of pregnancy, e.g. movements and positions to reverse a breech presentation or, during labour, to turn a posterior presentation; those aimed at familiarising and desensitising the woman to pain to assist her in its management during labour and delivery, e.g. calf stretches (mimicking uterine contractions) continued to the point of real discomfort; exercises intended to alleviate pain in labour, e.g. positions of childbirth (kneeling, squatting, knee-chest etc.), massage points, rocking, etc.; exercises aimed at strengthening parts of the body directly affected in childbirth, e.g. perineal stretches and pelvic floor toning; exercises aimed at assisting post-natal recovery of muscles stressed in pregnancy and/or birth, e.g. abdominal exercises; more general exercises to encourage the return of the pre-pregnant figure, e.g. to "work off" fat laid down during pregnancy on hips, thighs etc.; exercises aimed at "educating" muscles that will be used especially post-natally: upper arm (carrying baby), back, neck (tension, incline of head during breastfeeding) etc.; and finally, relaxation exercises practiced during pregnancy, post-natally, and in the course of labour.

In ante-natal classes it is emphasised that these exercises are not sufficient alone. While the exercises need to be done regularly at home as well as in class, pregnant women are also advised to maintain (or establish) a program of general fitness exercise, such as swimming or walking, to be undertaken three or four times a week. More liberal readings of pregnancy, then, expand pregnancy to take over the body; the body is subsumed by pregnancy. While the obstetric model holds to a uterocentric view of pregnancy (with its main practices centering on the diagnosis and treatment of possible problems), liberal/alternative philosophies include in their central regime of preparation emphases on separate bodily parts—feet, legs, thighs, abdomen, back, neck—each part of the body a part of a machine that must be coached and worked in order to build up its fitness, endurance and suitability for labour.

Exercise is only part of the preparation for labour. Women are supposed to gain a general familiarity with the processes of pregnancy, birth and delivery through informed reading and attendance at ante-natal classes. Here they learn a variety of techniques for the management of pain during childbirth, are encouraged to devise a birth plan including details of "prepping" and positions for first and second stage of labour, as well as express their wishes regarding analgesia, anaesthesia and various interventions such as induction, episiotomy, and the cutting of the cord. Nutrition during pregnancy is also part of the preparatory process.

TIMELY PREPARATIONS

A decade ago advocates of childbirth education spoke of the child-bearing year—one that included the three post-natal months as well as the nine months of pregnancy. To-day the time-frame is nearer to eighteen months, as increasingly women are urged to prepare for conception as well as for childbirth. The manual *Pregnancy, Birth and the Next Six Months* (1987) is exemplary of this approach.

In anticipation of conception women are advised to avoid events and activities regarded as stressful, such as moving house or changing employment; to give up nicotine, alcohol and various medications; to avoid dieting that might result in vitamin deficiencies possibly indicated in congenital malformations and to avoid vitamin supplements because of the risk of toxicity through over-dosage; to eat well (a healthy diet is set out); to have a dental check-up and a rubella test; to clear up any fungal infections, throat and urinary tract infections and appendix irritations and to attend to varicose veins; to cease contraceptive use of the Pill or IUD some three to four months before the projected conception takes place, and to shift to the temperature method for temporary fertility control. Finally, the pre-pregnant woman is advised to check that any prescribed medication is not contraindicated in pregnancy: "You can give your baby the best start in life by ensuring that you are as healthy as possible before you conceive" (p.6). The strictness of this regime is maintained throughout pregnancy and any slip, of course, may provide the *post factum* explanation of difficulties with the pregnancy or problems of foetal/infant health.

These prescriptions also apply to prospective fathers. For example, Blackmore's *Nature and Health Journal* (Hardy-Wardrop, 1978:39) encourages men to limit alcohol and nicotine, to avoid overeating and the use of narcotics, and to eat special foods that "bring strength": almonds, pine kernels, hearts of sunflower seeds and roasted sesame seeds, black olives and raw honey. This article also refers to caffeine as "one of the greatest mutagens to man" (ibid.), affecting sperm cells and the reproductive cells of the unborn.

Once women are pregnant, the self-surveillance recommended in many of the popular booklets and pamphlets is extraordinary. They are extolled to "give baby the best start in life" by planning the pregnancy and adhering to a range of dietary, behavioural and psychological prescriptions in line with the idea that "a happy and worry-free, healthy pregnancy will add to that joy and lay the ground-work for a contented baby" (ibid.). As with birth, "failures" in pregnancy and in the health of the infant are clearly attributable: women who do not work hard enough (i.e. follow the prescriptions and proscriptions of pre-conception and pregnancy) may be punished by miscarriage or a disabled or ill infant.

In addition to health and fitness, therefore, women are urged to modify their behaviour in other ways in order to prepare fully for childbirth and motherhood. In *Pregnancy, Birth and the Next Six Months* (1987), for example, in the fifth month of pregnancy, first-time pregnant women are urged to contact a woman with a small baby and to spend a morning or afternoon with her: "Watch her with the baby, cuddle the baby yourself and try to become used to handling this small person. You will probably feel very tender towards the baby." In the sixth month, women are advised to organise a network with other expectant mothers, thereby setting up a support system for the early and often isolating months of new motherhood. In the ninth month, it is suggested that women keep a kickchart, daily recording foetal activity:

> This lets you know the baby's sleep and awake periods, and may be useful later on if your baby is overdue. If a baby is staying in the uterus for too long, the placenta will fail and the baby will not be nourished properly, and its movements will diminish over a few days and then gradually stop. If you were keeping a daily foetal movement chart, you would be able to see this diminishing of movements and alert your doctor (1987:28).

In addition, women are enjoined to "give more loving attention" to themselves and to have a beautiful pregnancy, looking after their skin, face, hair, stretch-marks, diet, sleep and relaxation. In general, such prescriptive recommendations draw their persuasive power from their association with birth and its supreme importance; as one popular journal states: "Childbirth is the most radical experience of any woman's life and, with the right preparation, can be the most rewarding, too" (*Woman's Day* 23 September 1985:69).

HERSELF IN CONTROL

Thus all parts of the body become parts of the machinery of reproduction and a "proper" pregnancy is done through attention to and surveillance of all those parts of the body. These prescriptions are not peculiar to Australia, of course. Reproduction is, Romalis notes (1981:9), "too important to be left to the whims of nature";[28] in any society prescriptions and proscriptions exist which seek to control the processes of reproduction to ensure the health of both the mother and infant. Variations in the prescriptions and taboos of pregnancy operate regionally and between classes as well as between cultures but all are designed in some way to establish a measure of cultural control over pregnancy, to ensure the wellbeing of the foetus and a safe birth and confinement. Homans (1982), for instance, describes the range of behavioural proscriptions observed by British women that include dancing, lifting, and stretching which might precipitate miscarriage; "bad" thoughts and emotions that might be transferred *in utero* to the unborn; dietary proscriptions on potatoes, fried and fatty foods that could cause heartburn; and alcohol, smoking and "violent sex". For some, failure to adhere to these proscriptions carries a heavy moral portent: "Perhaps those women who do not stop smoking or drinking have not yet been transformed by that sense of responsibility for the child" and do not yet "believe in" the child or their ability to affect it (Bergum, 1989:86). The women in our study were of course influenced by these warnings and prescriptions, and modified their behaviour accordingly:

---

28. Note the irony of this statement in the context of the general emphasis on the "natural" in relation to birth.

I've read everything about tetrogenic substances, I've gone off the most ordinary foods because there is some kind of suspicion in the mind of some doctor somewhere who wrote something...but ultimately you don't really know. So, then probably someone who's really complacent about it and smokes cigarettes and knocks back headache pills and has a few grogs and things like that might produce just as normal a baby. But I don't know. It's a kind of religious ritual I'm going through, I suppose (Hilary).

And Linda:

I don't smoke anyway so I didn't have to worry about that but I haven't really had any alcohol, I mean I can't say I haven't touched it, but taking into account sips and things maybe I've had a total of two glasses over the whole nine months. And that's because I think that there is not enough known about it, one suspects that is might affect things like skintone and hair and that kind of thing. And the same with coffee...I've had an occasional cup of coffee, you know just a little bit, just to add flavour, that's been because of the effects caffeine is supposed to have. And I've taken, in a haphazard way, taken some vitamin tablets and some cod liver oil and, of course, iron tablets...I read a little bit but I haven't been obsessively interested in it.

There is, of course, nothing wrong with encouraging women to cease smoking, to avoid alcohol and other drugs, to eat well and exercise regularly. But the behavioural and dietary prescriptions as well as those specifically related to pregnancy and preparation for childbirth constitute also the moral environment of reproduction. These prescriptions are the means towards a goal of "natural", pain-free labour, an unproblematic delivery, a healthy baby and an easy embarkation on motherhood, and thus any deviation (resort to drugs during labour, an episiotomy, difficulties with breast-feeding, congenital abnormalities, an unhappy baby) may be regarded as a result of a slip in the preparatory regime. The regime is so comprehensive and extensive that slips are almost inevitable, but the recognition of this fact does not enable a woman to sidestep allocation of blame if she still believes in the efficacy of the regime itself. Therein lies the risk of this re-centering of the responsibility on the pregnant woman herself and away from her obstetric practitioner.

The foetal kick-chart is a case in point: it has been the role of the obstetrician to monitor foetal well-being, and late foetal death has not been attributable to maternal negligence. By suggesting that women monitor daily foetal movement, the locus of responsibility shifts: it becomes the woman's task to identify any deviation from the norm, to recognise when deviation signals abnormality, and to seek medical assistance. Foetal death then may be seen as the fault of the woman, when she fails to identify until too late the indications of foetal stress. This general shift of responsibility onto the woman brings in its wake her vulnerability to any variation of outcome. For many women, too, previous experience of miscarriage renders them especially vulnerable to these messages and dependent on the technological reassurances of foetal well-being. Vanessa, for example, had had a number of prior miscarriages: "I tried to calm things down so that hopefully this would work out properly. I didn't rush around and tell people like I had done with the others. I had an ultrasound at fourteen weeks and when that was confirmed I accepted it."

Hilary made a similar comment of the importance of ultrasound in confirming the viability of her pregnancy:

> I haven't had much confidence about the pregnancy; I've only been able to take one step at a time. I couldn't, for instance, I couldn't wear any maternity clothes until I was over 12 weeks and rather fat, for in relinquishing control I almost regressed into some kind of superstitious state. And there were other little signposts ... my mother got all this gear, this white gear (for the baby), and um I couldn't even look at it until I'd had the ultrasound ... I didn't really dare contemplate (having the baby) until the ultrasound.

TO HAVE A NORMAL BABY

Miscarriage results in terrible disappointment and pain for the expectant parents. "The pain of reproductive loss", Rapp (1988b:106) writes, "is universal" (see also Oakley, McPherson and Roberts, 1984). Women we interviewed found it hard to accommodate losses from miscarriage and felt that their womanhood was in question as a consequence (see Chapter 5 below). But the fear of giving birth to a disabled child is, past the first trimester, the major concern for women and the major factor that explains their dedication to pregnancy prescriptions thereafter: "The main worry I have is that the baby might be deformed. I think I'd try to trace it back to the first two or three months when you might not know you're pregnant and it's hard to do the right thing" (Penny).[29] Prescriptions surrounding conception and pregnancy thus prey upon women's fears that they may not give birth to a "normal" healthy child. The women we interviewed stressed the way in which fears of abnormality haunted them at times. They were scared that the baby "was a monster or something" (Hilary), and had "terrible dreams about her being abnormal" (Joan):

You actually think about it (giving birth to an abnormal child) quite a lot, and you just sort of hope it doesn't happen (to you) ... especially when you smoke and maybe have a drink or something, everything you do makes you feel quite guilty ... yeah, and the relief when it comes out and it's alright, it's quite overwhelming actually. I don't know, I think it's one of the first things that (my husband) said—Oh god, thank god it's alright. He was quite surprised (Helen).

And another informant:

I think everybody whether they admit it or not, there's just a little question mark at the back of your mind, but from the ultrasound, certainly you can see a lot more of the bits, the bits and pieces and they are all there and working so who knows (Anne).

---

29.   Considering the still extreme example of the United States where children may (and do) sue their mothers for *in utero* negligence that can result in say, congenital abnormality, the birth of a child with a physical or mental handicap can no longer be constructed as an exigency of "nature", since it is the thwarting of this "nature" which is seen to lead to aberrations. Preventive practices thus must be instituted to allow "nature" to produce the good result.

The birth of a normal child is not necessarily the only aim with respect to outcome. Future desirable characteristics of the child are also at stake and are seen to be dependent to some extent on preparatory practices, such as, for example, abundant oxygen intake of the pregnant mother in relation to the intelligence of her child.

CONTRIVING THE NATURAL

One can easily envisage a future in which a menu of practices during pregnancy (as well as before it) will be available to aid the development of a desirable personality profile for one's offspring. The months of conception and pregnancy are a period of ideological as well as practical training leading to the final performance, the components of which affirm the ideology, validate the efforts of the practice and, with their magic elements, attempt to influence the future. Within the activities directed towards this production, the ideological emphasis on the "natural" has led to the quite contradictory prominence of contrivance and artifice in efforts directed towards unadulterated labour. In this respect, reproduction is truly a child of its times, a product of modernity and its oppositional tendencies of formal rationalisation of actions on the one hand, and, on the other, the generation of semi-mystical forms to contain these actions. Thus nature pure and simple—in the sense of spontaneous activity in its ordinary environment—has very little to do with childbearing.

In the context of reproduction a set of goals is established, defined by a philosophy which disavows the technical rationality of the medical model of birth. At the same time, however, these goals imply prescriptions regarding a comprehensive set of defined, goal-directed behaviours for the actors concerned. Each pregnant woman, treating her body as a machine, works on discrete parts of this machine in order to optimise their functions and efficiency, thus seeking to render her pregnancy unproblematic and the birth successful—not only in terms of infant and maternal health but also in terms of purity of procedure which is expected to lead to immaculate parturition. Her relationship with the developing embryo is mechanistically constructed since any failure by the woman to adhere to the proscriptions and prescriptions of pregnancy (and pre-conception) may result in a deficiency in the final product. In this process nature is turned into culture and biological processes manipulated in order to counter the encroachment of technical rationality on the "natural" processes of birth. Thus the ideological dimensions of birth and pre-birth *praxis*, which stress the spontaneity and directness of the "natural" process, are in direct contrast with the salient characteristics of the practices which they inform and advocate. The fact that this paradoxical situation has existed for some time is due to two circumstances: firstly, the factually eclectic behaviour of women (not always, as we have seen, in accord with their beliefs) makes it possible to transfer the inconsistencies of the ideological model to the actions of its target population and, therefore, to press further for the continuous promulgation of it. Secondly—and more fundamentally— the model's images are significant metaphors for social circumstances far more general than the vicissitudes of childbearing which they depict. For both of these reasons, the model has a high degree of functional independence from the actions which it purports to influence.

BODILY WAYS

The way in which individual women themselves perceive their bodies is often at variance with the cultural representations of the process of belabouring the pregnant body. One of the striking aspects of our findings concerned the holistic manner in which women experienced changes in their body and related this to the changing social status and their relationship to their partner. Often a number of images, and associated themes, operated concordantly—the body as host to the foetus, the body as sexual object, the body as a vehicle for communication with the partner. The articulation of women's thoughts about their bodies and the effects of pregnancy on them is reflected in various other works on pregnancy. Bergum (1989:56, 57), for example, writes of the nature of the pregnant body as vessel "for containment and nourishment of an other (which) transforms the woman to mother" and speaks of "the desire of women to express their own strength and excitement and wonder at this time of intense and radical change". Bergum associates the clothing of the body in maternity wear as the outer symbolling of the body as container, and a mechanism that moves women towards their greater awareness of "the bodily presence of the child" and their steps towards becoming a mother.

The women in our study were not so romantic, and indeed were sometimes ambivalent about the physical changes that were part of pregnancy, uncertain of their ability to idealise an infant in this context, and questioning the significance of this in terms of their relationships—with their husbands as well as others. In Chapter 5, we return to this theme and examine the way in which women speak of their bodies as containers, as a means of understanding pregnancy in relation to their unborn child. It is clear, however, that the changing body shape is important to women as public proof of their changing status, and this is because of the way in which the pregnant body is viewed by others. Excerpts from interview texts illustrate this well. Women spoke of their own images of their body:

> I've been quite vain about it (my body) really...It's just one of those things, you now, where the pregnant woman thinks she's the only woman in the world who's ever been pregnant and what a wonderful thing it is (Linda).

> It's a big thing these days to feel that if you're going to have a baby you're not as trendy as those who don't. When I was pregnant there's such a stereotype, I felt people were looking at me. I used to get indignant when I got on buses and people didn't give me a seat...but when I started to have that pregnant shape I loved it. I just liked being pregnant; I'm a terrible show-off. When I had her I thought, I must have another one now (Joan).

And of their husbands: "He thought a pregnant body was rather beautiful" (Marian); "he was very proud of it—he was always trying to get me to put on big dresses even when I wasn't showing and things like that" (Beverly). But on the other hand:

> (My husband) couldn't bear to touch my stomach in the late stages of pregnancy because of the violent movements. He was interested in the changing shape; he couldn't stand the thought of it happening to him. He didn't know what to expect either, but I'd read a lot at night and he seemed quite interested in that (Carolyn).

The pregnant body is also a symbolic force in wider social relations—with other kin, and outsiders. Women noticed the way in which expectations and assumptions of their behaviour and abilities shifted with their increased belly and their changing status. They noted the ways in which others who had already had children used the appearance of pregnancy as a means to initiate conversation and effectively to incorporate the pregnant woman into a world of parenting and children:

> My mother-in-law felt I should change my personality...well, the fact that I fell pregnant just proved you know that there was some hope left, and the fact that I no longer felt comfortable in jeans so I took to wearing dresses was wonderful...she thinks it's rosy now I'm pregnant. Other people too get real clucky about it ... a lot of people treat you differently because you're pregnant, especially people I don't know are a lot more talkative. Like friends of my husband's family. I think it's because they think there's something to talk about...they become so chatty, you know: Oh, when's the baby due? What are you hoping for? What are you going to call it? Are you feeling well?—the usual questions, but it's nice you know...a motherly kind of reaction (Jennie).

> One of our friends loves pregnant women so he's been very protective. And mothers and mothers-in-law relate in a completely different way...they couldn't really talk to me before, but now they certainly can relate to me in a field where they are the experts. They feel they can intrude more into your personal life (Penny).

The people I was working with...it was good because they used to make comments about my shape and—I can't describe it. They just made silly comments all the time but it never really bothered me because most of the time they were just joking. Because I worked mainly with men and so they were comparing it with what their wives went through I suppose, and giving me hints, helpful little hints all the time (Carolyn).

PARTNERSHIP CHANGES

While women spoke of a general easiness in their relationship with their partners through pregnancy, and, on the whole, men seemed comfortable with the physical changes in the women, there was a certain ambivalence concerning sex. Women's interest in and experience of sex during pregnancy varied greatly. In some cases, women's desire diminished during pregnancy; in other cases fear of precipitating a miscarriage or "hurting the baby" affected continuing intercourse, particularly with penetration:

He seems a lot more like interested in personal contact and stuff and seems more interested in me now. Like I've found sex very hard since I've been pregnant and I've always been a very tense sort of person and since I've been pregnant I think I've worried a lot about if the baby will be alright. So I've avoided sex sort of thing and he'll kind of stay clear, so things have cooled down a lot there. But he's much more affectionate...comes up and gives me a cuddle (Jennie).

It's had ups and downs. I've become less interested in sex. Partly this was because in the first month, we had intercourse around about the time I would've normally had a period and I just had a little show of blood and I think that made me a bit nervous...I've become a bit more interested in sex again, but really I've wanted lots of cuddles and affection and everything, partly because I sort of see that it's...one doesn't look very lovely really. But he hasn't been...some men might get very irritated by all that, but it's been sort of alright (Linda).

In other cases men's equivocation in face of their partner's pregnancy impeded desire:

> He isn't really as accepting of the process as I'd like him to be. He's found...you know how you get veins (showing) in your breasts when you're pregnant...well, he doesn't like to look at those funny veins. I don't feel that I am desexualised but he does feel that to a degree. So it's rather sad for him; he can't really go along with female sexuality, he can't really share in it. He has to follow at his own pace, and from about the 26th week...I was very pregnant then, and the veins were out. I think it was the veins more than anything else (Hilary).

We have noted earlier the role of the father in childbirth and, in anticipation of this, prescriptions in behaviour, analogous to those applied to women, which operate for men prior to conception. In addition, a new couple-related model of childbirth has also demanded the integration of men through pregnancy, with respect both to the emotional investment of men in the pregnancy and to their practical involvement in its processes. The above interview-texts imply that this is not entirely problem-free, at least not for all men. Thus Hilary commented to us of her husband's view of pregnancy:

> It just made him squeamish to think that there was something alive inside me. I think it might have been a milestone when he first felt it (move). When he did ultimately feel it he didn't say anything, but it seemed to have quite an influence on his feelings. He started watching me too in a funny way...watching the transformation taking place in me, maybe.

In the popular literature that is concerned with social fatherhood, pregnancy is portrayed as an emotional turning point for men as well as women. The literature emphasises the redefinition of the couple with conception and in the course of pregnancy, as a moment of significance in the history of the couple. Indeed, this is represented in the frequent use of the term "pregnant couple", in contrast to "pregnant woman" who is addressed in a lot of childbirth educational literature. Women themselves recognise the transition to a relationship that is ushered by a child:

> I didn't really know what, how it was going to change our life, I didn't really want it to change our lives because we are quite happy the way we live now and we don't have all the interruptions that parents seem to have, but in some important way I felt that it would help us accept our own mortality and help us grow old gracefully. And I, we do know some people who don't have children, who made a conscious decision not to have children, and I don't want to be that way (Hilary).

All women shared this sense of change. "Once the baby arrives," Margaret commented, "things will never be the same; there'll never ever be just the two of us again I feel a bit regretful. Even when they've left home, it still won't be the same as the very beginning".
And Bronwyn:

> In a way, it's saying goodbye to part of your relationship, and I think that it's a big thing to give up; I don't think people look at it from that aspect enough. It's a bit insulting in a way, it's like saying to your partner, I've had enough of just the two of us, because you'll never have that again if you're realistic—like you'll never have the spontaneity of being able to just do things.

EXPECTANT FATHERS

Women's perception of the impact of pregnancy in transforming social relationships, particularly from that of couple to the creation of family, or a couple-with-child, is a theme that also dominates much of the popular literature. The focus in recent years on the role of men in, and their reactions to, the social and emotional aspects of reproduction, is in part a reaction to the individualism of modern motherhood, a means of maintaining the notion of couple, hence also of family, in face of a counterforce which positions the woman centrally in the contemporary problematic of having children, or at least gives far more attention to the mother/

child dyad than to husband/wife, or to a two-parent family "unit". As the women we worked with observed, this is a complex situation. An article published in 1981, for instance, notes that:

> Before pregnancy she (the pregnant woman) may have been fulfilled in her relationship with her partner but generally sooner or later, love, intimacy and the warmth of this relationship, physical satisfaction and fulfilment in the 'couple' will develop into a more mature wish to create and fulfil biological and procreative roles. The long held belief about being a parent—a father or mother, about being fertile will find fruition in wanting to have a baby and the reassurance that comes from discovering one's fertility. For so many, becoming pregnant is confirmation of the secure relationship, the proof of fertile sexuality and of choosing a future together...the couple is now a triad, a threesome, a family (*Parents and Children Magazine* 2:21)

Notably, "being a parent" and "wanting to have a baby" come, for both fathers and mothers, before "becoming a triad" and, lastly, "a family". This echoes our earlier discussion (in Chapter 2) of "having a child" as a correlate of the increasing individualism in relation to the significance of motherhood—or, in the present instance, parenthood.

In this text the differences between men and women are minimised, and it is presumed that the expectations, values, ideals and roles of both are related to common understandings of love, sex and fertility. This contrasts with the usual representations of sexual difference in Australian society, as well as elsewhere. Not all popular journals share this presumption, although most articles available in this medium begin with a supposition that women feel like this, that is, that reproduction is a natural and desirable outcome of a stable sexual relationship for women. Where popular writers perceive different rather than common goals of men and women, they emphasise the responsibility of women in maintaining the coherence of the couple in the face of the potential competition of a child:

Natural birth with father assisting brings both parents closer to an understanding of the meaning and realisation of true union. Birth is one of the closest emotional, spiritual moments that can possibly be shared by a man and a woman ... Unfortunately many men feel, and women allow them to feel, far removed from the moment of conception, and so they view the experience of pregnancy with detachment...If you genuinely want to share this miraculous experience then he will sense it, and the sharing will grow and include the ultimate act (i.e. birth) (Hardy-Wardrop, 1978:39).

This is, in fact, a relatively early text, but its tone, and the general philosophical arguments, are sustained over the next decade in the popular literature which has reflected interests in academic writing related to women and motherhood. Thus during the mid 1980s, the literature generated by the renewed interest in reproduction among feminists was concerned with the dilemmas of combining motherhood and work and with the impact of pregnancy and parenthood on their lives. Men also began to address this issue from an academic perspective (Russell, 1983; Callan, 1985). Not surprisingly then, the popular literature on fatherhood again reflected this concern. The *Parents and Children Magazine* for instance, in an article on "Pregnancy: the first feeling of being a father", is concerned with the "difficult task of becoming a father" following confirmation of pregnancy:

A lot is expected of a man once it is certain a baby is on the way. He is supposed to be proud and happy, and must burst with understanding for his partner and always show her consideration—for nine months. He is supposed to put up lovingly with her emotional ups and downs, yet often enough he himself is in emotional turmoil...His wife is the centre of attention. No-one talks about his problems and yet what problems they are! The feeling of being 'caught', of having no more freedom. The wonderful holidays as a couple are over. Sporting activities which he may have to give up. The zippy little car which will have to be replaced by a sturdy family wagon... And how will their sexual relationship be? He has heard rumours about no sex for months. What is he supposed to do then? have cold showers or will his desire automatically diminish in accordance with her reduced interest? And his paternal role: what sort of father will he be? (*Parents and Children Magazine* Aug/Sept 1986:48).

Although we have quoted this article at some length with implied irony, it was not written with that intent, of course. There are a number of possible ways of reading the text, including the way in which it reflects real and voiced concerns of some men whose partners may be pregnant for the first time. But one can also detect a thinly veiled misogyny disguised as insight into male ambivalence regarding pregnancy, as the article seeks to elicit female sympathy for male equivocation and to render the woman responsible for mediating feelings of exclusion, rejection and entrapment (and self-indulgence) the man might experience.

The article continues to draw out an extraordinary analogue of male and female emotional states during pregnancy. Thus not only women need to adjust to their pregnancy through a shift in emphasis from changed reproductive status ("I am pregnant") to anticipated changed social status ("I am going to have a baby") but so too do men pass from the recognition of reproduction ("my partner is pregnant") to changed social status ("I am going to be a father"). However, the writer warns, men may find this transition harder than do women, "for regardless of his involvement and all his joy, he remains feeling an 'outsider'. The baby is a mystery to him although he can sometimes feel its movements if his partner calls him at 'the right moment'." He is erotically marginalised also: "the larger the tummy grows, the more definite the feeling becomes in lovemaking: someone has literally come between us" (ibid.). Practical steps are offered to women to minimise this sense of male marginality: his attendance at any ultrasound; a joint visit to the maternity hospital or birth centre; his introduction to the obstetrician and midwives prior to labour; and the choice of hospital that will allow his presence at a Caesarian section, should this be the eventual outcome, or at least the right to care for the infant immediately after the operation.

In this view, taking care of the pregnant father can become yet another task for the pregnant woman. Not only is she responsible for the health and welfare of the foetus, for her own health and

fitness and quality of the birth experience, but she also has to facilitate the transition of her relationship—from couple to family—
and, within that, to foster the precarious ability of her partner to
become, socially, a father. Constant vigilance and hard work are
therefore her lot throughout this period of preparation for the twin
birth she is to accomplish: of her infant and of her family.

JUST REWARDS

Our analysis in this chapter can be taken a step further: an interesting parallel can be drawn here with Weber's thesis concerning
the Protestant ethic and its puritanism, in both actions and values,
deed and thought, that allied itself powerfully to the development
of modern capitalism. This puritanism was the result, Weber
asserted (1958), of a desire to demonstrate, through righteousness
in all its manifestations, rightful predestination; in this process the
development of capitalism was the unintended consequence, so to
speak. In an analogous fashion, the assiduous pre-natal and parturition practices of women labouring within the "natural" value-
and belief-orientation are meant to ensure a mode of birth which,
in any case, has already been laid down by Nature as both the
"normal" and "good" destination of pregnancy. In both cases hard
work, vigilance and observance of strict standards of behaviour
have originated as means to an end and have subsequently become
ends in themselves. This has been rendered possible—indeed,
inevitable—through the association of these practices with a
morally defined goal preordained as such by a superior—transcen-
dental—force (God or Nature, as the case may be).

In the fullness of time, the puritanism of early capitalists has
blossomed forth into a manifold of fetishisms of post-industrial
society. It could well be that a similar process leads from the strict
ante-natal and birthing regimes of the "natural" philosophy to a
view—and carefully stage-managed experience—of the "good
birth" as a desirable commodity, a status-symbol, a necessary
enhancement of the modern "minimal self" (Lasch, 1985),
impoverished and fragmented as it is by the very practices which

are designed to enhance it. Here we might heed Weber's unease concerning the ultimate irrationalities of rationalised actions and wonder if the body itself, controlled by "specialists without spirit, sensualists without heart" (Weber, 1958:185), would in this process not be turned into an iron cage to imprison the human soul.

Chapter 5

BONDING, SOONER OR LATER

This chapter is concerned with the development of love for and attachment to the newborn, the course of the establishment of an emotional tie usually referred to as "bonding". We have already noted that becoming a mother is not a singular event but a process, one spanning the months of pregnancy, childbirth and the puerperium. Physiologically this process is clear, marked at the outset by the moment of conception and at the conclusion by the return of the uterus to its near pre-pregnant state. Psychologically, the prolonged period of pregnancy allows for a gradual adjustment to the notion of motherhood and provides women with time to anticipate the practical and emotional impact of the beginning of parenthood. The relatively predictable duration of pregnancy provides a determinate framework within which these accommodations can take place. Indeed, among women in our study, a number who gave birth earlier or later than the expected date of confinement were confused and often distressed by this changed timing, as it curtailed their internal projections of the necessary period of adjustment and their reactions within it. In every way—biologically as well as socially and emotionally—birth is the high point of the process of becoming a mother.

As we have argued in earlier chapters, this high point carries a great deal of cultural significance and its essential dramatic impact is emphasised through elaboration and ritual as the culmination of the process. However, it is a high point only. In most respects, the period after delivery is even more important for mothers, for it is during this time that the birth experience is reviewed and integrated with women's concepts of themselves, while, at the same time, emotional and practical adjustments are made to accommodate the real presence of the new infant. In addition, the investment of self is much greater, in so far as the post-natal period involves effort and vigilance over a significantly longer time (and often with much less assistance) than do labour and delivery. Since at least the mid-1970s, the central concept in relation to this period—denoting, for some, its most important function—has been "bonding", the establishment of the indelible tie of attachment and love between mother and infant.

TENTATIVE BEGINNINGS

The women in our study gave varying responses concerning the actual timing of the initial development of this bond with the infant. For some, it began as early as their first knowledge of conception; for many of these women, it was preceded by the anticipation of conception and was related to their decision to bear a child. For them, failure to conceive or miscarriage resulted in considerable grief: one woman spoke of her bitter disappointment with each menstrual period—particularly if late, even by a day or two—for six years until she finally conceived in her late 30s. For others, their first emotional response to the foetus was at the time of "quickening"; still others felt the baby was "real" only after the birth. Differences in the time at which women believed that attachment had begun were partly due to the extent to which they were able to focus on the pregnancy and to visualise the developing foetus; partly also to their confidence in the outcome of the pregnancy and their belief that at the end of it all there would be a live and healthy baby to love. Women who identified in themselves the early establishment of bonding often spoke of a transition in their awareness, expressed by them as a shift from "being pregnant"—essentially a description of their biological status—to "having a baby", a phrase that encompassed their emotional and social commitment to the pregnancy and the forthcoming infant. This transition was often associated with a significant moment when the baby became "real" for the first time: this might be the first felt movements of the foetus, or the first glimpses of it on the screen at the time of an ultrasound. Along these lines, Bergum (1989:53, 55) formulates phenomenologically the key experience of pregnancy: "being with child moves a woman to motherhood in a unique fashion...it is the process of becoming what one already is".

In this connection, our interview material supports the trend identified by Judith Lumley (1980) that women give the status of personhood to the foetus at an increased rate in advanced pregnancy. In her study, 30 percent (of 30 Australian women giving birth to their first child) thought of the foetus as a "real person" towards the end of the first trimester, whilst 90 percent of her sample did so at 36 weeks. In our group, Margaret, for example, associated changes in her emotions with her awareness of foetal activity well into the second half of her pregnancy:

> I felt definite movements of the baby at around 30 weeks or so and for the first time I really believed I was having a baby, at an emotional as well intellectual level. It's been very much academic till then. I still can't really believe I'll have a real live baby at the end. When I was first pregnant, I'd follow its progress—'it gets fingers on this month' and so on—and to that extent it's always been a baby— but mostly I've felt 'I'm pregnant' rather than 'I'm having a baby'.

Knowledge of foetal development informed women's growing awareness of and commitment to the unborn child. Sue and Jill, for example, both identified the beginnings of their emotional commitment with the transition from embryo to foetus status, the point when they understood the possibility of miscarriage had diminished and they felt able to invest emotionally in the pregnancy and to anticipate the birth of the baby. For Sue, quickening was a further landmark in the emotional history of her pregnancy. For Jill, an ultrasound at 14 weeks then movement at 17 weeks reinforced an earlier emotional bond:

> I think I developed it (a relationship with the baby) very early. I used
> to talk to him all the time, especially going to work. I don't know
> why it was going to work and coming back home; I suppose it was
> because it was just us. I'd say 'Right, we're going off to work now'
> and all that rubbish ...And then later on, the last couple of months,
> whenever he'd move, I'd always give him a little pat, play with him.
> I couldn't wait to see him.

For Jane, ultrasound gave her a sense of the substantiality of her pregnancy, as well as helping her to prepare emotionally and cognitively for the outcome. "It was good for me to see it more as a baby, apart from me, rather than just having it there...being able to look at it perhaps more objectively. It's all very well carting it around for nine months, but I think it's quite a change (once the baby is born)". Her response was not dissimilar from another woman's reaction at first sight of her newborn: "Hello, little baby. Now I've got to believe in you" (*Sydney Morning Herald*, 4 September 1986:15). Women's comments about the role of ultrasound in giving substance to the personhood of the foetus are reminiscent too of the experiences of American women, for whom the technology of ultrasound, foetal monitoring and so on provides the evidence of pregnancy, the "technological confirmation outside of her own intrabody awareness that a pregnancy does, indeed, exist" (Michaelson, 1988a:11).

Other women, however, were unable or unwilling to give material reality to their infants during pregnancy, even at times to accept that they were pregnant and would have a baby. This is captured succinctly in Jan's reaction to her delivery of her son: "Look, it's a baby!". In Bronwyn's case, difficulty in conceiving over a two year period led to disbelief when the pregnancy was confirmed, which continued to the time of our interview, a few days after the due day of birth when labour had not yet been established:

> The last month has been pretty awful, when everybody is saying
> 'Oh, isn't it wonderful, aren't you getting excited', and you just feel
> like crying, and...I don't give a stuff. I feel a bit guilty—it's hard to
> feel a lot, you know, to get a relationship with the baby. People sort

of tend to put a lot of their own ideas onto you, and you often don't feel that way. You're carrying this medicine ball around…sometimes I still find it hard to think it's anything more than just a sort of sore leg or something, just a part of me. I guess when it moves a lot…you're feeling absolutely horrific and it's keeping you awake at night, you feel quite negative to it…You can't relate to it. (You think) you must be a monstrous person if you don't feel loving to the baby (but) it's quite a big adjustment. I think pregnancy must be the most stressful thing anybody goes through. Now I still think 'Oh, it's probably not even a baby in there'.

Similarly, Jane recalled:

When they were doing the ultrasound they…at one stage they were trying to get a measurement across the baby's head and…you could see the little baby turning its head and its little nose sticking up…a little thing looking through a whole layer of amniotic fluid and flesh and everything else…it's only really shadows. But it was good, I mean it was good for me to perhaps see it more as a baby, apart from me rather than having it there…it's sort of a bit hard to think of this bump as being a little person. It's like carting a boulder around. Turning it into a little person is a bit different.

Like Bronwyn and Jane, Jennie found it difficult to accept her pregnancy and give concrete reality to the forthcoming infant and to identify any emotional commitment to the infant prior to its birth. Two weeks before her son was born:

I didn't really feel pregnant until a month ago…I felt no different at all and wasn't until I had trouble sleeping that it actually kind of hit. It's taken me a really long time to accept the fact that I'm going to have a baby…I'm not even sure now that it is, you know, one hundred percent real. Like I kind of think 'I'd better get that done before the baby comes' and 'I wish Jim could be at home this week so that we could spend a bit of time together 'cause we won't be able to after the baby comes', but the actual fact that there is a little creature coming…I can't really imagine a baby.

DOUBTS AND MISGIVINGS

Women spoke to us expressing concern regarding the "proper" development of their maternal feelings. Any perceived deviation in the expected pattern signalled possible difficulties in the future relationship between the mother and child, and abnormality of the woman herself: "Someone at work asked me if I had any maternal feelings when I was twelve weeks (pregnant) and I didn't have any and I wondered if I was normal" (Penny). At the same time, they also resisted the manner in which others projected emotional meanings onto the pregnancy: "You do less thinking about it than other people; they say 'you're having a baby' versus (you think) 'I'm pregnant'" (Jo).

For some women, emotional hesitation towards the foetus, or an inability to ascribe to it personhood, had its origin in prior experiences associated with fear of loss of the infant. Jo, for example, related her emotional distance during her pregnancy to the experience of a friend who had had a stillbirth and whose present pregnancy was threatening to miscarry. Jo had had an ultrasound early because of a suspected ectopic pregnancy, and she had prepared herself then for an abortion. To the end of the pregnancy, she maintained a stance of emotional distance: "I don't feel I am personally attached although I'd be terribly upset if something went wrong...I haven't been getting myself too attached to any picture of it (the baby)".

Women with a history of miscarriage most often spoke of emotional distance. Sandra, for example, had been admitted to hospital the previous year at ten weeks, and had spent ten days there before finally miscarrying. At the time of the miscarriage, she said she treated the episode relatively objectively. But at the time of our first interview, when she was 22 weeks pregnant, she looked back on it as the loss of baby, and found the actual miscarriage—the passing of the embryo into a bedpan—distressing: "It's not fair. No-one, not even a foetus, deserves to be treated that way". She had kept a diary during that first pregnancy but had not done so this second time in order to avoid the emotional investment that this might have represented or caused, and which might have led to greater distress should this pregnancy too have resulted in loss. In her mind, she marked off each week as a milestone towards the probability of having a child and looked to the 28th week of pregnancy as the time when she believed the pregnancy was viable, and when she felt she could relax and begin to anticipate the arrival of an infant. Similarly, Barbara, after two miscarriages, had attempted to remain emotionally distanced, but had failed and had become so anxious about her present pregnancy also resulting in a miscarriage that she was finally referred to and received psychiatric counselling: "I wasn't going to allow myself to become attached to this baby. I'd completely distanced myself...(but) within a couple of months I was completely wrapped up in her and knew it would destroy me if I lost her. One or two spurts of blood at fourteen weeks and I went into hysterics; I thought I was going to lose her then".

Not all women who were especially fearful of loss did so on the basis of prior miscarriage:

> I've been a bit reluctant to think about (the baby) because I haven't had so much confidence about the pregnancy. I've only been able to take one step at a time... in relinquishing control I almost regressed into some kind of superstitious state and felt, you know, if I do this then that is going to happen...My mother got all this baby gear but I couldn't really look at it because I hadn't had the ultrasound, but even now I am not very happy about looking at it and letting whatever effect it's supposed to have on me happen (Hilary).

The theme of superstition of which Hilary is so aware can be discerned in the attitude of other women towards practical preparations for the baby's arrival. Linda, one week before her expected date of delivery, comments, "I've just decided I don't want to think about all of this stuff too much ahead. I haven't been interested in that kind of thing at all and I think that it's the lack of knowledge (that) is protection".

Women who eagerly anticipated their infants and who established an emotional attachment early most often spoke of their *in utero* infant as a "baby" or used a nickname for it. In contrast, women who remained distant tended to refer to the foetus or their pregnant bellies as a "lump", a "bump", a "thing", a "medicine ball", or a "little parasite" (cf. Breen 1975:161), and maintained an aloofness from their pregnancies. This recalls Martin's findings among American women who also present several images which indicate a marked sense of separation of self from the body, a passive approach to it that is also sustained through labour and delivery (Martin, 1987). These women commonly spoke of the physical costs of childbearing, their anticipated loss of selfhood as a concomitant of motherhood, and of the end of their unique, exclusive relationship with their partner:

> That's what surprised me so much about being pregnant. Like I got this real feeling of being a host, you know; (it's) a parasitic sort of thing, it's really weird but that's how you feel. But I mean it's not horrible...I think that there's always been this two-way thing, a sort of conflict between wanting to still be my own person and knowing that I've got to give myself up for this child. I've got to more or less suppress myself...at least for a few years (Helen).

LOVE AT FIRST SIGHT?

Regardless of their attitude during pregnancy, most women presumed that "bonding" would be instantaneous at the moment of delivery and were caught by surprise and sometimes distress when this experience did not eventuate in its perfect form. Both scientific and popular literature have given considerable attention to "bonding" at birth; it is as the result of this that many women are confused by their emotions at birth and the lack of correspondence between their expectations and the reality of their feelings. The popular literature especially emphasises the importance of the first minutes of life. Mutrym, for example, writing in *New Parent*, argues that "interference" in childbirth (i.e. Caesarean section) may result in difficulties that "endure for months or even years following the birth and may, at least initially, impede optimum psychosocial development of the infant," as well as affecting the mother's "thoughts and feelings about this infant" (Mutrym, 1985:28). Others similarly emphasise the importance of mother-child interactions during the first hours after birth in initiating the maternal (or parental) bond and in establishing nurturing responses. Bowley (1985), presenting a summary of some of the scientific literature in the *Breastfeeding Review*, writes of the preconception, antenatal, intrapartum and postpartum periods, in addition to the early days after birth, as distinct psychological and social as well as biologically distinct times when bonding may be negatively affected or enhanced, depending on circumstances.

Academic writers have by now largely revoked notions of the crucial importance of the first moments, for, as Jan Pilgrim argues, "to concentrate the burden of a lifetime of emotional commitment and growth into one hour puts an intolerable strain on parents. If they miss that hour, what are they to do then?" (Pilgrim, 1984b:28; see also Richards, 1985:293-4). However, in our group, women whose labours, delivery and recovery failed to match their expectations and who had to accept greater obstetric intervention than they anticipated or regarded as desirable, were particularly likely to be concerned that the "bonding process" had been impaired; and that, as a consequence of this impairment, their relationship with their child had been placed in jeopardy. Other women were surprised at the absence of great emotion, an expected surge of maternal love at first sight. Subsequently many would attribute this to some procedural deficiency during delivery, some contamination of the occasion that interfered with the perfect setting required for bonding to take place.

Of course, some women did have the experience of "falling in love" with their infant:

I'd say it took me about 24 hours for my mind to merge the baby that I had kicking inside me with the baby that I had in the cot beside me—these two images slowly came together over 24–48 hours. I suppose the first overwhelming feelings were the first night, when I wanted to feed him...when they brought him to me, when I'd been asleep recovering a bit, and there he was, these two little eyes peering at me in the darkness, and that's when I remember thinking 'God I love you; you are the most wonderful human being in the whole world'. And I've never stopped feeling like that (Jill).

But others, including women who felt greatly attached to their infants *in utero*, found it difficult to deal psychologically with their newborns. In many cases physical exhaustion from labour and delivery impeded any sense of active pleasure, even of interest, in the newborn, and in interviews women often spoke of emotional dissociation that continued for some time after birth:

> I remember him (husband) saying 'It's a little boy, darling', and I felt no real sensations; I just felt 'Oh, thank goodness it's over'. I couldn't believe anything could be so rough. I remember feeling really happy, but I can't say I felt any great maternal feelings until the next morning...but at that time (i.e. of delivery) I was so whacked I couldn't appreciate very much at all (Denise).

> I was glad that it (childbirth) was over. I was tired and I guess I was excited but it did not feel as though the baby was mine. I did not feel a big gush of love. It wasn't exactly a let-down but it did not seem real. During the pregnancy I'd feel the baby kicking and I was very excited. Then when the baby was born it didn't feel real, but that might be because of what you've just been through. You're not really straight and you're feeling a little bit tired...I didn't really feel this bonding straight off. The baby didn't feel like it was mine. I didn't even feel I wanted to nurse it; all I wanted was a cup of tea and a wash (Carolyn).

Carolyn was only one of many women who did not feel that the newborn baby was hers. Other women felt ambivalent or disassociated from their new born (cf. Breen, 1975:163). Those whose infants were receiving intensive care were most likely to feel apart from their newborn, but others too, for whom childbirth had been relatively unproblematic and whose babies were with them, also felt remote. "Immediately after the birth I wondered if this was my baby", Lorraine recalled, "I asked Nick if he felt like a parent and neither of us did...In the first hours there was not a lot of attachment. That grew as time went on". And Laurie commented that

> I didn't really feel like cuddling her. I felt rather sorry for her because, you know, there was this little thing...like wet putty...I just

patted her, I didn't feel like hugging her close...I really just wanted to go to sleep. (Bonding) took weeks actually.

Many women were able to identify a later timing of the commencement of attachment. Hilary felt that her love for Claire began on the third day:

> That's when I started crying because I couldn't believe that I was going to have her...I felt I didn't have the opportunity to be myself after the baby was born. There were lots of people coming in every day and interrupting feeding schedules—I found it exhausting. I suppose on that third day I did a lot of weeping because she was everything I had hoped for and had been too frightened to hope for...I couldn't believe it that I had got my little girl.

Other women thought that the process of attachment took considerable time:

> (Bonding) means being able to feel that she is part of you. I think the bonding is the part when you say: 'That's my beautiful baby', and not just 'That's a beautiful baby'. It took at least a couple of weeks. You feel very lost even though you've done a lot of reading and been to classes. It takes a while to work out what the baby wants (Joan).

Confidence in being able to look after the infant was frequently associated with attachment and mother's responsiveness to the baby:

> I didn't feel much in the first few days—there was so much going on and anyway it was such a surprise. So for me it was feeling OK about her and her settling in a bit. I think it's the feeling that you can cope and that you do really like the baby...When a baby really smiles, after weeks of drudgery, that really keeps you going (Julie).

> (Bonding began) when she first started to respond with her smiles. Before that it was hard slog... but I never actually resented it—I knew it just had to be done (Heather).

The establishment of an early reciprocal social relationship—
that is, as evident through smiling—is important in these texts,
and other women spoke too of the significance of their infant's
smiles in sustaining them during the early weeks: "The loving
comes naturally, but the caring doesn't...But you get through it
even though you think you won't. At six weeks it decides it will
smile at you and all the pain is forgotten" (Zoe).

In general, "bonding" was considered to occur at the same time
that a woman became aware of "feeling maternal". But in
recounting to us the process of the development of love, women
also related maternal feelings to their behaviour: gazing at the
infant, stroking it, breastfeeding:

> Even though I did not feel maternal before or at the birth, after-
> wards I felt very maternal. They put her on my stomach and I really
> wanted to breastfeed her then. But I have read that there is doubt
> that there is, in fact, such a sensitive time (for bonding) and I was
> so tired right after the birth...(I) had to send a message to have
> Sophie (the baby) taken away (Marian).

Marian's familiarity with the debate concerning bonding is not
atypical. Most of our informants read voraciously about maternity
and mothering. Even the most common sources of information—
tabloid newspapers and popular women's magazines—provided
them with a vocabulary to discuss the psychology of mothering, as
well as to build up a set of expectations that derived from this. The
degree of self-consciousness about their emotions was striking in
interviews. Women anticipated and expected to "feel maternal"
and to "bond" with their infants, usually at birth, and to be able
to incorporate their newborn infants immediately into their lives.
They were concerned and distressed when the emotions of mothering proved as difficult or as problematic as its more practical
tasks. But in some cases, the difficult tasks of the everyday care of
the infant, and its perceived fragility and vulnerability, clouded out
other feelings. Vanessa, for instance, maintained that bonding and
love happened when the baby began to "do things" at six weeks—
to smile, lift her head, and so on. But she continued:

She was probably three months when I started to feel close to her instead of frustrated and anxious, and being frightened of her waking up in those first few weeks...I felt very uncertain and I am sure a young baby senses this. Because she was so small I felt so frightened and (my husband) felt the same. A couple of afternoons I felt totally lost, I went out and slammed the door and left her screaming. I also used to escape down the street when I could be sure she was sleeping.

HOW DO I LOVE THEE?

There appears to be considerable variation in the patterns of new mothers' attachment to their infants and in the development of their love for them. Indeed, as the above extracts from interviews indicate, "attachment" and "love" in themselves are shorthand terms which denote a variety of emotions, reactions and perceptions. In all probability, the pattern is determined in a very complex fashion by the interaction between, on the one hand, individual psychological characteristics, especially in regard to affective responsiveness (with respect to which there can be wide individual variations) and, on the other, social circumstances and physical factors at the time of birth, as well as thereafter. We observed, for example, that many of the women whose attachment to their infants developed slowly, had physically difficult birth experiences. Of the women quoted above, Joan and Laurie had relatively easy and intervention-free births, but Laurie was exceptional in a different sense as she had to adjust to twin daughters. Julie gave birth at 36 weeks and her daughter was ill for several weeks afterwards, spending most of her early days in hospital. Hilary and Heather were delivered by Caesarean section, in both cases a few weeks before their due dates. Both were hard hit by baby blues while in hospital, though in neither case did they suffer post-partum depression subsequently.

There is a considerable body of literature on the impact of Caesarean delivery on bonding. Mutrym (1985:28-32), for example, argues that post-partum separation of mother and infant, because of anaesthesia of the mother and hospital routine whereby the infant is placed under observation, affects the mother's acceptance of the infant (see also Lomas, 1966; Breen, 1975:168). Mutrym (1985:28–29) further notes that first contact often occurs when the mother is feeling pain or distress, and when she is having difficulties in integrating her actual experiences of birth with the planned or fantasised event, this having a negative effect on her feeling for the infant.

In general, amongst our informants, women whose births were unproblematic, who required little or no medical assistance and who had immediate and unbroken access to their infants, most readily spoke of intense, early feelings towards their babies. Conversely, difficult and disappointing experiences in labour were associated with reported difficulties in adjustment and attachment immediately after birth. At the same time, there is no evidence in our findings that, in the longer run (e.g. several days after birth) difficult birth experiences interfered significantly with the development of love and attachment between mothers and infants. As one informant put is, a few days after (Caesarean) delivery: "Just because birth went wrong, I don't think the bonding went wrong; bonding includes being with her".

One of the oversimplifications involved in the concept of "bonding" is the failure to distinguish, as our respondents' accounts clearly do, between the highly charged emotional experience of the sudden rush of feeling for the newborn (not necessarily experienced by all women), and the gradual development of attachment and love for the infant that may only slowly seep into consciousness in ways which vary considerably from woman to woman.[30] Our study suggests that the surge of feeling at birth is neither a "natural" part of labour (even where the mode of delivery is entirely "natural"), nor a pre-condition for the growth of maternal feelings over time. Nevertheless, the idea of "bonding" is part of the modern folklore about birth and many women feel disappointment and guilt in relation to the perceived shortcomings

---

30. Individuals differ greatly in their perceptions and understandings of love and attachment, due to both personal historical and psychological factors (M.M. Kaplan, 1992).

of their own birth experience and their accomplishments in this respect.

NURTURING AND NURSING

In the day-by-day process of caring for the baby, feeding has a special place and is of special concern for the new mother. A number of issues arise out of women's concerns with this activity. Most of these will be discussed in the following chapter; in this chapter we shall focus mostly on those aspects of feeding which relate directly to women's conscious awareness of attachment to their new infants. Here breastfeeding is of greatest importance—it is an issue that arouses some of the strongest emotions and questions regarding patterns of feeding, its duration and quality, as well as the appropriate time for weaning, preoccupy most women during the early months and weeks of motherhood.

The great majority of women in our group breastfed their infants, at least initially. Women believed that "breast is best" for newborn infants; all women planned to breastfeed their infants for some time. Their desire to breastfeed was influenced by the "naturalness" of the process, the nutritional appropriateness of breastmilk for infants, and psychological factors—a belief that breastfeeding was an important means to establish "bonding" and attachment between mother and child:

> Breastmilk has properties in it that helps the baby fight infection plus…it's so convenient. I think it's also nice to have the closeness with the baby, to have the baby close to your skin and *vice versa* (Joan).

> I think if you're fit and healthy, it's good…for the mother as well as for the child, kind of gives you, gives you more of a bond sort of thing, makes you feel closer to the kid, but if I wasn't 100 percent healthy I wouldn't be doing it, because I don't think it's good to pass on anything you've got to the kid…if I had to take drugs or was feeling as though I wasn't doing the best thing for the kid, I'd be

bottle-feeding. It wouldn't really upset me if I couldn't, like if my milk did not come through or something (Jennie).

From Jennie's last sentence we can also glean the significance for women of their ability to breastfeed as a kind of index of a "natural", "proper" motherhood. This notion is also held by Hilary who stresses the importance of breastfeeding:

With myself, I was bonded to her by three weeks. I feel very fortunate to have been able to breastfeed, being a Caesarean. It was very important to me to breastfeed having been denied a proper childbirth. I was about the 24th person to touch my child probably (after the birth). I don't like the thought of weaning because it's going to separate her and me in some way.

The sense of unease about bottle-feeding in Hilary's last sentence and the superiority of breastfeeding in comparison to it—particularly in emotional terms—is also evident in the following extract:

I like to give my attention to him while I am feeding him—I like to have that eye to eye contact. But you can do that just as easily with the bottle. (But) it (breastfeeding) is more important to me than I could ever have imagined it would be. I'd be very disappointed if I had to put him on the bottle now—it makes me feel special to him and really important. I feel really happy when I am feeding him, that he is enjoying, that I am giving him something that he needs and loves—such an integral part of his growth (Amy).

The strength of feeling associated with breastfeeding for Amy surfaced in an incident which she described thus:

A girlfriend was down with her baby a couple of weeks ago and wanted to try him on her breast and I always thought wet-nursing was a great idea. But I was really upset when she did it. (Why?) It hit me that maybe I wasn't all that necessary for him at the moment. It was only for a couple of minutes, but I was really surprised by the feelings I had. That was a real revelation to me, that I felt that strongly. I mean, she is my best friend…she went to put him on and

I said, look, he won't like it. At first he nibbles it and I said, look he doesn't like it—it was terrible. It was certainly jealousy on my part.

Not all women would agree about the importance of breast-feeding in bonding, of course. Denise, who fed her child only for six weeks, felt that it was important initially: "I think it's important but also I think you can make up for it. I really feel that the first six weeks were important. I wouldn't want to put a baby straight on the bottle".

In contrast, Julie, who also breastfed for six weeks only, felt that breastfeeding was not an essential element for bonding: "I think that bonding with the feeding is in the holding". The role of touching in the relationship with the baby is also stressed by Roberta:

We had a great interdependence, I would have hated to stop feeding her for some medical reason...it was nice. I think it was the sensa-tion and the touch for her and the feel...that's why even while you're holding onto her and giving her a bottle you'll see she might be kneading at my hair or touching your arm—just touch. She's very dependent on touch.

By contrast to working-class women who generally referred to a five to six month period of breastfeeding, the middle-class women in our study tended to anticipate longer periods of breastfeeding and to adopt a more liberal approach to extended nursing, at least partly because of the psychological benefits seen to be associated with it. For some, this attitude quite explicitly tied in with an appreciation of the more "natural" approaches in other cultures. Linda recounted, "The most secure person I ever met is a chap who was breastfed until he was six ...by various wet nurses (in India). Extraordinarily secure person. And I think that that's due to breastfeeding. ...I quite like the idea of weaning it (baby) from the breast to the cup but I'm not quite sure at what age"; and Hilary believed "I feel I should feed for as long as possible, prefer-ably at least a year. ...In Papua New Guinea they're still breast-feeding sometimes at three or four and everywhere you go where there are local people there's always a couple of breasts out and babies or young children sucking from them".

Most women felt that breastfeeding, and/or the contact with the baby during it, automatically ensured closeness between themselves and their infants. Conversely, many felt that the comparative lack of contact created a distance between fathers and their babies; for example:

> The father is just not so involved in the child all the time, I mean the baby obviously responds to me and responded to me very quickly, whereas he did not respond to (husband) in the same way, very early on....he (baby) was responding to me positively, and he obviously had a preference for me, I suppose purely because I am breastfeeding him, and because he sees me all the time (Helen).

MALE BONDING

Since fathers have increasingly become an integral part of the social processes of birth, it is not surprising that, over the decade, their ability to bond with their infants has also been rendered problematic. Indeed, it is more so, since they have not carried the infant and have a far more limited notion of the embodied infant: hence the emphasis in some popular parenthood manuals on the father's speaking through the mother's stomach walls, so that the foetus might grow accustomed to two voices rather than one, the emphasis of paternal presence at ultrasounds and foetal monitoring, of feeling the baby kick, and so on. We had not initially chosen to explore paternal emotion, but our informants themselves raised the issue of the attachment of father and child. This links with our earlier discussion of the incorporation of men into the event of birth, providing women with personal and practical support but also enabling bonding of both parents to the newborn according to a model that places primacy on the experiences immediately following delivery.

Research remains inconclusive regarding the importance of fathers' attendance at birth, early contact with the infant and bonding (Palkovitz, 1985), although it is significant that a substantial body of literature has developed around this issue (e.g. Greenberg and Morris, 1974; MacFarlane, 1977; Phillips and Anzalone, 1978); and, as Palkovitz notes, the public does believe that attendance at birth is an important factor for fathers and the development of their feelings toward the child. The women in our study largely shared this view. Margaret, for example, was concerned that her husband be present at the birth in order to enhance his attachment to the baby as well as to "witness the pain": "It'll be an emotional time for us, binding the two of us together and bonding us as three. They keep talking of birth and bonding between the baby and the mother, and never about the father, but it must be as important, as crucial, and it's got to be done at the same time if possible".

Some women felt that their husbands bonded more quickly that they themselves did, since the men were not exhausted or dazed from analgesics. Carolyn felt that "It was more real then for him than for me...I think he had more of that feeling (of bonding) than I did. He's very close to her now and maybe it had something to do with it, and Denise said of her partner "He has always been very calm, and that's how he was the whole time (throughout labour). I think he enjoyed the baby a lot better. He could appreciate the baby straight away, whereas I was too tired".

Other women, however, felt that their husbands had limited emotional ties with their babies for some weeks or even months. Husbands were proud of their new infants but rarely participated extensively in childrearing, especially while the babies were physically small and were only breastfed. Jane, for example, felt that her husband remained aloof from his daughter until she was around five months old; Hilary felt her husband bonded with their daughter at around three months, although "the process still goes on". In speaking of bonding, women also constantly alluded to their advantage over their husbands through breastfeeding as a continual means of attachment between mother and infant.

SACRED TEXTS

The term "bonding" is relatively new. The usage and indexing of it in standard textbooks dates from the late 1970s, clearly following the publication of *Maternal–Infant Bonding* (Klaus and Kennell, 1976). Following Kuhn's (1970) contention that propositions relating to accepted paradigms are to be found in standard text-books, we have located a telling reference to the concept of "bonding" in the 11th edition of a well-established textbook of pediatrics:

> Whether there are critical periods generally for the establishment of optimal mother-infant relationship in humans…is not fully resolved. There is much to suggest that some losses of opportunities for making the most comfortable and harmonious conditions for interaction between infants and their families may be irretrievable within hours of days after the birth of the infant (Nelson *et al.*, 1979: 19).

The crucial aspect of the bonding theory is therefore the "critical (or sensitive) period" and not the formation of the bond itself, the inevitability of which (given the "right" circumstances) is in fact tacitly taken for granted.

A great deal of experimental and clinical evidence for the sensitive period was put forward by Klaus and Kennell (1976), on the basis of which they argued that conditions governing contact between mother and infant during this time might affect decisively a woman's feelings and actions towards the infant in the weeks and months to follow and thus have consequences for the baby's development in the long run.

The "bonding" theory made its appearance shortly after comprehensive criticisms of obstetric practice had begun to have an effect on both consumers and practitioners. Thus timing probably was responsible, at least in part, for the rapid acceptance of both the theory of "bonding" and the use of the concept itself in the further questioning of hospital birth-procedures (e.g. Kitzinger, 1979). Couched as it was in scientific and biological terms, bonding theory was also acceptable to the medical profession—

and, specifically, to obstetricians and paediatricians—to the extent that the theory and its applications became a strong factor in many improvements in hospitals which, in the last decade or so, made labour ward routines, in general, less rigid and their atmosphere more human and therefore, presumably, more attractive to women.[31] Ironically, this same belief in "bonding" has also resulted, as we have seen, in much maternal anxiety and guilt since at least the late 1970s.

It must be noted that in their broad sense, the ideas expressed by the bonding theory are by no means new. In 1953, for example, Moncrief and Evan (1953:61) argued that "the relations established between mother and child during the early days and weeks of life set a pattern which may be of value for the later development of the child". But what distinguishes the contemporary "bonding" theory is its emphasis on the concept of the "sensitive period" and its crucial importance for the formation of the affective tie between mother and child.

Since its early days, the bonding theory has been subject to much controversy in professional circles (Lamb, 1982; Klaus and Kennell, 1982, 1983; DeVries, 1984; Marsh, 1985). Nevertheless the popular literature seems to have accepted unquestioningly its implications for the importance of the early cementing of the relationship between mother and infant (Kitzinger, 1979; Welburn, 1980). The influence of this literature appears to have been widespread as, for example, in the skin-to-skin contact between mother and baby immediately after birth which is almost *de rigueur* in current popular models of the "good" birth. In all probability, the contemporary accounts of the "heady experience of birth" (Maynard, 1986) and the emphasis on its importance and its ecstatic nature, have contributed to the swift promotion of the concept of "bonding" as a necessary component of the event. In Australia there has been a proliferation of magazines concerning

---

31. Arney (1989) argued that the bonding theory was, in fact, socially and politically useful to the medical profession and health care institutions in that it provided an appealing (and necessary) rationale for substantial changes without which these institutions might not have survived the criticisms mounted against them at the time.

birth and early parenthood and these abound with personal accounts of births which probably serve as models for the event. For example: "He (the baby) was lifted on my tummy, so warm and slippery...We were left alone for over an hour which was a special and precious time...I lay on the delivery table and cried tears of delighted relief because...all my dreams had come true and I had a new life to love" (*Parents and Children Magazine*, 1986: 80).

REVISIONS AND REINTERPRETATIONS

Thus it seems that public attitudes have not been influenced by the fact that less than a decade after the publication of their original influential work on bonding, Klaus and Kennell (1982) have revised of their earlier, much less equivocal, views on the process:

> Studies have not clarified how much of the effect may be apportioned to the first hours (after birth) and how much to the first days, but it would appear that additional contact in both periods will probably help mothers become attached to their babies...although there is increasing evidence from many studies of a sensitive period...this does not imply that every mother and father develop a close tie to their infant within a few minutes of first contact. Each parent does not react in a standard or predictable fashion to the multiple environmental influences that occur during this period (Klaus and Kennell, 1982:56).

Klaus and Kennell's last words on this subject are quite significant for our discussion:

> Although birthing practices may have become more humane because of the impact of research on this topic, it is unfortunate that the quality of care may have been compromised inadvertently in some cases because of a lack of understanding of all the studies of bonding. Our current concepts of early as well as extended contact are a matter of record: 'Obviously in spite of a record of early contact experience by mothers in hospital births over the past 20 or

30 years, almost all these parents have become bonded to their babies. The humans are highly adaptable, and there are many fail-safe routes to attachment. Sadly, some parents who missed the bonding experience have felt that all was lost for their future relationship. This was (and is) completely incorrect'.

And:

Some misinterpretation of studies in this area may have resulted from a too literal acceptance of the word bonding and so has suggested that the speed of this reaction resembles that of epoxy materials. We have also been concerned about feelings of guilt and failure on the part of high-risk mothers (Klaus and Kennell, 1983:575).

In their present form the views of Klaus and Kennell are, in fact, not very different from those put forward by Bowlby in relation to his well-known—and by now somewhat infamous—concept of "maternal deprivation" (Bowlby, 1953, 1969). However, the potential for pejorative implications of Bowlby's key term, in conjunction with his emphasis on the prolonged duration of the process of the "growth of love", has removed his ideas from the agenda of the popular contemporary discourse. By contrast, the (mis)interpretation of "bonding" as a sudden, crucial and necessary part of the "good birth" in both its experiential and procedural aspects, has widespread appeal. We contend that part of the reason for this appeal may be the perceived potential of bonding to secure the instant accomplishment of attachment, the long-term requirements of which cannot necessarily be assumed to be forthcoming. Since an increasing number of women is actively engaged outside the home, perhaps the vulgar versions of Bowlby's ideas, intertwined with traditional images of motherhood, still fan smouldering anxieties and guilts which may, then, be warded off with the magic of instantaneous bonding.

Implicit in the work on bonding there is also a set of conservative ideological suppositions about motherhood, tacit values of the educated middle class and heterosexual models of proper parenting. As Arney (1989) argues, bonding theory, as a resurrected and scientifically reformulated version of the "maternal instinct", has been used as yet another means by which women are kept in their place.

At the same time, other interests are enmeshed with this position. According to De Vries (1984), for example, bonding theory gave the medical profession a medical rationale to change obstetric practices in line with the demands from groups that were advocating natural childbirth. Thus the bonding theory allowed the timely assimilation of consumer demands into medical organisations, displaying, "like other innovations in medical practice...a tendency to move from an ideal expressed by a few patients to a regimen imposed on all" (De Vries, 1984:99). The most obvious danger of this generalisation, as we have already argued, is in the idea that early separation leads to irreparable damage to the mother-infant relationship, thus causing unnecessary guilt and anxiety. But the concept of bonding also excludes considerations of adaptability and compensation that are general characteristics of the developmental process. It "encourages us to ignore the complexities of human relationships. ...Where is the space for the ambivalence that is universal (in them)—for the joy, fear, anxiety, frustration, triumph, and many other feelings we may have for our offspring?" (Richards, M.R.M., 1985:294).

BEHOLDEN TO THE BABY

Prevailing cultural images are not always reflected in specific individuals' actions and feelings, although they may well dominate their awareness. It is simply the case that the term "bonding" is widely used by women to refer, in a short-hand sort of way, to the development of feelings towards their infants during the first few weeks after birth, as well as to the early and sudden feeling of overwhelming attachment and love which some women experience. But precisely because of this usage, "bonding" as a concept has become reified and coerces, in the sense in which Durkheim (1964) used the term, most women, regardless of the quality and circumstances of their own experience, to believe and expect that something distinct and recognisable will emerge in the first hours or days of motherhood and that this special event will place a permanent emotional seal on their relationship with their infants. When describing their own feelings and reactions in detail, however, the new mothers who spoke to us of their early experiences with their babies acknowledged that the feeling of "love" did not necessarily surface until some time after the birth (although it might "pop up" in brief moments earlier). They also knew that the sense of responsibility towards, and a strongly felt need for vigilance over, the baby, were feelings that were present in their consciousness from the very start.

Rather than employ the umbrella term "bonding" to describe all these developments, we would like to propose a more complex account of them: the earliest emotional state of motherhood is that of being beholden to the infant. This state is expressed operationally in a variety of ways of caring, as well as in more negative expressions of it, such as anxiety and doubt. A self-conscious feeling of attachment and love, on the other hand, is a qualitatively different emotion which often develops later and is not merely a further elaboration of the state of being beholden, but rather a new and additional dimension. Within this broad pattern, many individual variations are possible in a process which lasts a lifetime as attachment to babies over the years necessarily changes into partial disengagement from adolescents and finally—hopefully— friendship with one's adult offspring. In the later phases too love is as ubiquitous an accompaniment of mothering as it is in the period of intense, close-range care given to infants, though it may not be experienced and expressed in the same way. In the life-long condition of motherhood change is the only constant; no pattern of action and no emotion is permanently bonded onto its structure or universally applicable to all women.

Chapter 6

FEELING DOWN BUT KEEPING AFLOAT AFTER THE BIRTH

> I did not know motherhood was so demanding; there are no classes
> for being a parent (Natasha).

Natasha's feelings were echoed by all our respondents. While birth
might have been disappointing for some of them, they all knew, in
general, what to expect (hence, in some cases, the disappointment) and were at least partly prepared for what was to come.
Birth, however difficult and arduous, is also a finite experience and
all women, the regrets and disappointments of many of them
notwithstanding, have some feeling of accomplishment after the
event, even if it is only in the limited sense of having seen it
through, one way or another. Similarly, pregnancy is a largely
chartered process of limited—and also, in this case, predictable—
duration, within which women can play an active, autonomous
and controllable part, however hard they may need to work at their
chosen tasks.

But caring for the new baby is a different matter altogether. It is
continuous, ever-present, demanding and unpredictable.
Compared with the routine work of pregnancy, the toiling of
motherhood is unscheduled and often consists of coping with
circumstances as they arise. It is laden with responsibility and, in

135

most cases, socially isolating and lacking adequate supports. Thus many women feel vulnerable, lonely and confused most of the time and all women feel some or all of these things some of the time.[32]

EARLY PROBLEMS

Women's concerns with the care of their new infants often centre on feeding. Difficulties in relation to this may start very early, frequently in the hospital:

> When Adrian was first born and I put him on the breast, a trainee nurse came in—a male—and I asked him what to do. He told me ten minutes on either side and I got a cracked nipple out of that...I had to work out for myself how to posture feed him (Lorraine).

> I was demand-feeding at the hospital, but there was not enough support...There is too much conflicting information, especially about breastfeeding; either 'try to get baby to attach' or 'leave him alone'; 'take off your bra' or 'never take off your bra'—it made me feel horrible (Janet).

Janet also had cracked nipples at the start of breastfeeding and had to express for three days which "made me feel horrible". She felt that there was not much emotional support at the hospital for her condition. Other women shared with her a feeling that hospitals provided inadequate support and care: "There is not enough understanding at the hospital...I was not allowed to supplement the feeds even though I was reasonably sure that I did not have enough milk—so in the end it was onto the bottle for him after five weeks" (Gillian).

---

32. This is by no means a recent development. Dyer (1963) for example, suggested that most couples experienced severe and extensive crisis with the birth of their first child, although the scope and duration of the crisis varied according to a number of personal and social factors.

The dilemmas and anxieties that arise immediately postpartum, and especially with respect to feeding, were common among the women with whom we worked. Marie, for example, was 44 when her daughter was born by Caesarean section. She was very keen to breastfeed and eventually managed to do so for 8 weeks, but it was not easy at the beginning: "Just as well I am not very young—I would get intimidated and bullied about child-care (by the nurses). Yet there is often contradictory information given, especially about breastfeeding. Some are trying to help me...but this nurse favours bottle-feeding...she makes me feel self-conscious and incompetent" (Marie).

Liliana's account of her early hospital experience is particularly significant, as she was subsequently to wean earlier than planned and to change her mind about breastfeeding "one hundred percent":

> Every time they brought him to me in hospital to feed him, I'd get really upset and uptight, because I wasn't doing the right thing according to the hospital. ...I had so much trouble at first...Like when they first brought him, my attitude was OK, here's the baby, put the baby on the breast, the baby will now suck, everything will be fine, but it's not like that at all...he was all dopey and he wasn't sucking properly; my breasts were... absolutely engorged and he...kept slipping off...and then when the flow started he was drowning in it...and there wasn't anyone around to tell me what to do or how to do it or anything, just sort of trial and error. And then eventually I got him on three minutes each side and that was fine, I was empty, there was nothing left, this was just before all the milk came. But on their little chart I should have been up to ten minutes on each side...and the next day this dragon lady comes along and yells and stands there and makes me do it for ten minutes each side...I was in absolute agony with all this milk and I did not know what to do.

The above excerpts highlight the need for better training of professionals who attend mothers and infants. Such training has to include a renewed emphasis on the post-partum period from which, as we have argued earlier, the current dramatisation of birth has detracted attention.

Other women too spoke of a lack of understanding in hospital, of conflicting assessments of infant needs and women's need for information (e.g. reassurance that suckling would increase milk production in response to infant demand), of an absence of "emotional support", and the barrage of conflicting messages, as in the example of Janet, above. Of course, not all women were critical of hospital staff and the care and advice they received after they had delivered. In some cases new mothers gained confidence from nursing staff: "Two sisters helped a lot. There were ones, oh, in their thirties and they had had children themselves. I think they were the best help. They'd sort of explain things, and they sort of made you feel as if it was not just you" (Denise).

INEVITABLE UNCERTAINTY

Most women know, again from the literature on motherhood and infant-care, that breastfeeding is good for babies; most women enjoy it and get great emotional satisfaction from it. Once feeding is established—which is not difficult in most cases—and any problems like sore and cracked nipples are overcome, the activity itself generally proceeds quite smoothly. Its overall pattern, however, is often a cause for concern. Mothers do worry about the quantity and quality of their milk and are not comfortable with the easy dismissal these fears sometimes receive from doctors or baby health centre nurses. Women also worry about the timing of feeds, often not being sufficiently confident in demand-feeding ("is she really hungry when she cries—or is it something else?") but equally doubtful about the advisability of "scheduling" the feeds.

> I don't like breastfeeding. I never know whether she (the baby) has had enough. This is especially a complication of demand-feeding, which is just another fashion in hospitals at the moment. My mother was horrified when she heard about it...She (the baby) is always hungry; I find this very draining. But it is mainly the thought that I am it, everything for her—I find this overwhelming. The

whole thing is a difficult process. You watch the nipple, it slips out, the baby sucks air, you have to keep an eye on the watch...Demand feeding is inconvenient. I can't plan anything. Also, if the baby cries, is she hungry, or not? I am beginning to recognise the crying a little...but is she distressed when she cannot go to sleep? (Diana)

There are some important themes in this excerpt. The first concerns practical problems associated with feeding, in respect to which most mothers lack confidence, at least initially. Diana relied on what she had been taught at the hospital about breastfeeding and subsequently plodded on with the help of the baby health sister; clearly her doubts and anxieties were not dispelled by advice received from these sources. Associated with this theme—and the basis for its importance, in fact—is the "awesome responsibility" theme. All women we interviewed were aware of their central role in the infant's life and the significance of their caring activities, but some women were quite overwhelmed by the realisation they were literally maintaining their babies' lives.

This sense of commitment, obligation and responsibility extends for many women from the immediate moments of early infancy to the foreseeable future: "Just the fact that his whole life is sort of dependent on what I do and how I bring him up...that's something I worry about, we won't sort of live up to the task. There is so much involved in it. And it is gonna go on for a long time" (Helen).

Such perceptions and feelings, in turn, relate to the third theme which has to do with the need to be in control, especially in the case of feeding. Because this is so vital, most women feel that it is important to manage it well and, furthermore, to have some criteria by which to assess the results of their efforts. It is not only the vital importance of feeding, of course, which is the basis for this need. The nature of modern society and its patterns of everyday life instill in most persons expectations regarding the rationality, manageability and relative predictability of their various tasks (Berger *et al.*, 1974). Life with new-born babies is, in most cases, quite different, perhaps especially so for women previously accustomed, for some years perhaps, to a considerable measure of control over their activities in the workplace—as was the case with Diana, for example. It was for both of these reasons—the "awesome responsibility" and the "uncontrollability" of breastfeeding—that Diana was uncomfortable with demand-feeding which effectively undermined the possibility of order and planning not only of activities in relation to the baby, but everything else as well: housework, reading a book, visiting and, of course, eating and sleeping in a "normal" fashion herself. Many women share these feelings: "I demand-fed at first (in hospital) and now (4 weeks later) still do—but underlying is this wish that she would get with scheduling herself so that I can get my own life into order...also sleep! I face each day with apprehension: what is to-night going to bring?" (Rosemary).

Finally, the extract from Diana's protocol highlights the theme of the subtle institutional influences over breastfeeding. Here demand feeding, intended as the "natural" way to feed in contrast to the rigid schedule feeds that were popularised by Truby King (which had provided the regimen and moral philosophy followed by the previous generation of women; see Brown et al., 1943; Olssen, 1981), has been rendered problematic. Thus women are expected to intuit hunger accurately (where previously timed feeds neatly dictated hunger at four-hourly intervals); feel obliged to assess adequate milk consumption for an unspecified time-interval (where previously compensation would in any case be forthcoming in precisely four hours time); and are actively responsible for their infants health and development (where previously this development was not always causally connected with specific aspects of maternal behaviour such as feeding and stimulation).

Demand feeding is part of this whole process of being "tuned in" to the baby—and yet it is subject to external pressures and "objective criteria" (hence Diana's reference to "keeping an eye on the watch" to ensure equal sucking time on both breasts). Hence also preoccupations of many women with the appropriate posture for breastfeeding, with the right "atmosphere" of relaxation and calm, with their diets in relation to the quality of their milk etc. These concerns are not unreasonable in themselves; but the real point here is that modern demand feeding is far from being a "natural" activity as there is a body of appropriate knowledge from expert sources that is applied to it. It takes, it turns out, a particularly confident and relaxed new mother to master that which is alleged to come naturally.

The prescriptions of breastfeeding—the enculturation of the natural—are played out again in popular literature, including that of the NMAA (Nursing Mothers' Association of Australia) which contributes to a discourse on the "art" (or science?) of breastfeeding under the slogan of "the natural thing to do". Women's success too is monitored objectively through the Baby Health Centres, where initially on a weekly basis each baby is stripped, weighed and measured, often to the distress of both mother and infant. Good babies are those that grow the "right" amount of weight over a "proper period" of time: the ideal is one that, through the use of a statistical mean, sets each mother and her child in competition to that mean. Slow weight gain is taken as index of inadequate milk supply, and faced with inconsistent advice from baby health centre nurses, doctors, friends and mothers, women often shift to using bottles to monitor, precisely, infant milk consumption.

In the early days of mothering, the theme of loss of control, unpredictability and inconvenience is a common one. It shows up again in the following interview with a young (19 year old single mother) in circumstances quite different to those of Diana's: "This bedroom is starting to close in on me, I have not been anywhere for weeks...I enjoy breastfeeding, but it isn't convenient, I can't go anywhere. You can't be with others (friends) easily because they're not parents...I miss just being able to take off to the beach. Now the simplest thing has to be organised two days beforehand, and even so, it may fall through" (Rose).

Difficulties in organising or re-organising their lives around a small infant are connected with restriction of activity and loneliness. Maria noted "you are not free any more. It takes us an hour to get ready to go anywhere. It's more exacting for me. Everything seems a big event. I would like to go back to work, but it is not possible. There you meet other people...but here I only see one person".

OUT OF THIS WORLD

Lack of freedom, physical isolation and the contrast of these circumstances with the adult companionship enjoyed before the birth, both socially and at work—these were themes to which many women returned, and often they expressed a sense that they were not part of the "world". Motherhood and the "real world" of paid work and the company of other adults were presented in opposition. For most of these women the choice was clear: to be a real (and good) mother and not in the "real world"; or to be in the "real world" and a bad—or, at any rate, not a good—mother. Even the frustration of perceiving this dichotomy and of missing the contacts with adults that the world of work offered, was seen as evidence of their inadequacy as mothers: "I did not think I would go back to work but I'll go back part time. I can't see myself enter-taining a little baby all the time. I don't feel like a real mother—I feel just the same as I ever have" (Julie).

Indeed, as Helen suggests, feeling like a mother is precisely not to feel "part of the world": "You are in a different world. You do feel different physically of course…cos you feel different physically when you're pregnant… and when you have the baby, cos you've got all these things happening to you, but you also don't feel part of the world you know".

Sometimes this feeling was particularly acute in relation to the male partner and his greater freedom to move about in the world:

> I began to feel quite insecure in myself—what I was doing, because there he was going out into the world and there was me staying at home, washing nappies and things like that…it was the contrast of him going off… meeting people, all the things I used to do—I felt lost by seeing him going off. If I'd been on my own I probably would not have felt it (Pam).

This difference is perceived acutely; indeed women anticipated it during pregnancy, speaking to us of a need to adapt, to "isolate themselves" and get used to "not getting out and about" (Jane), and thereby to be a proper mother: "I wanna be a mother, like totally—give everything I can to my children. But I still wanna have a life of my own. Y'know, it's really hard" (Beverly).

Of course, not all mothers shared this view. Some were content; perhaps significantly, the following statement was made by one of our respondents from a country town:

> It's a different lifestyle altogether being at home and looking after a baby. I don't miss work, I don't want to go back. I go into the (workplace) and talk with my friends, but I don't miss it at all. I've got to go back in September and I'm not looking forward to it—I'm saying everything to get out of it. (He) wants me to go back for twelve months for financial reasons. I'm worried about the effect it will have on the baby. I think it's definite that I'll go back. If we have problems with the baby then I'll resign. I'll only work for twelve months and then I'll have another one (Natasha).

It is by now a sociological truism that the Industrial Revolution has split the social world into the private (home) and the public (work) domains which divide human existence under modern conditions.[33] Until relatively recently, women's lives were framed, as well as incarcerated, within the former, with motherhood merely adding the deadlock to the gates that had in any case kept them from entering the public sphere. The last three decades or so have ushered a change, however: increasingly women participate in the world of work and—more importantly (since many women have, in fact, always "worked" as servants, typists, dressmakers, governesses, prostitutes etc.)—in the work of the affairs of the world (though not in equal measure with men). Now the advent of motherhood does not seal women's fate of confinement within the traditionally sanctioned institutions of the private sphere, as it

---

33. This, of course, is an oversimplification. We recognise both the structural and ideological linkages between the two spheres through which aspects of the "public" world intrude into, and pattern, the "private" world—and are, in turn, re-inforced within the latter; gender relations represent a telling example of this situation. It is nevertheless valid to conceptualise two distinct spheres of *experience*, each characterised by its own specific styles of social interaction and subjective perceptions of conditions pertaining to them.

once did, amidst much general approval. Though being home-bound by an infant is even now, in practice, a common— but mostly temporary—condition of almost all new mothers, motherhood itself does not restrict any more the contemporary woman's existence (and her self-image) to the private sphere, since now her allegiances extend well beyond home and family life. Instead, maternity situates the split between the private and public domains within her being, in her heart and soul.

The intensification of the emotional life within the private sphere and the increasing emphasis on its passions and intimacies are closely bound up with increasing rationalisation in the public sphere (Van Vucht Tijssen, 1990). Both are aspects of modernisa- tion and jointly engender a personal life that, freed from tradi- tional institutionalised constraints, becomes attenuated and bereft of firm reference points, with meaning and stability being then sought in the inner self (Giddens, 1989:115). Thus any necessary negotiations between, on the one hand, the pressures from this nebulous, though passionate, domain and, on the other, the demands of the over-structured public arena, take place within the person. Women do not simply experience "conflict" or "role strain" or "loss" in this painful situation—though subjectively this is what they may feel. What they really manifest—or, rather, what is at the basis of their feelings—is the deep schism which is one of the fundamental dimensions of modern society and which cuts across the lives of all individuals in one way or another, though more deeply so, at present, in the case of women.

FEELING DOWN

During the period of early motherhood some women become quite distressed and their concerns become consequently magni- fied, creating a vicious circle of anxiety, dysfunction and depres- sion. For some, the narrowing of the social world concomitant with early mothering, and the range of new pressures concerning feeding and caring for the infant, push them to the edge. One woman wrote to us: "I felt isolated from the outside world, unable to cope and emotionally not very stable. Friends have since commented they have never seen me in such a state" (Alison). Other women expressed hopelessness and a sense of a loss of self:

> I thought I'd never really do anything again, that this was the end of life...now I'm starting to feel that other things are possible, that there is the possibility of doing other things as well...it's just (about) maintaining, I suppose maintaining my own identity, whatever that means ...that I am not just a body that other people draw from. You know, sometimes I used to feel that I was just a body, that um my body was the most important thing, that's what (the baby) survived on, he's taken everything out of me...I was just a body that had to perform these functions and that was that, I was not a person of my own, I wasn't an individual. And I sometimes just wanted to say, look, I'm an individual you know, I maintain a separate life all of my own. Quite often I just wanted to get away from it, you know, I just wanted to leave them and go away, be by myself for a while (Helen).

> I couldn't manage...my head was full of cotton-wool, and there was this horrible yawning feeling in my guts...sort of desolation, because there was this baby I had and I couldn't cope (Frieda).

In recent years, a number of both popular and academic writers have turned their attention to the subject of post-natal depression, its medical and social context, its possible long-term consequences for the women and their families, and the insufficient recognition the problem has received by the helping professions, both theoretically and in practice (Oakley, 1980; Welburn, 1983; Cox, 1986). It is not our intention to cover this ground again. However, the main findings and ideas of these authors need to be highlighted here: the isolation and lonely suffering of depressed new mothers, the frequent ignorance regarding both the ubiquity and the nature of this condition and the consequent shame and guilt which are experienced by the women so affected. These are all significant themes which are also echoed in our discussion, as they feature, in various forms and to varying degrees, in the accounts of most new mothers we have interviewed.

Here it must be noted that our approach differs somewhat from the usual clinical, practical and/or structural orientations to the subject. By contrast with these more "objective" approaches, in our discussion we focus on comprehending the content of the experience of depression during the post-partum and the subjective meaning of women's feelings. There is a sense in which, in the relevant professional literature, specific experiential components of depression are viewed as mere epi-phenomena. In this view, gut-wrenching feelings and anguished thoughts become manifestations of disorder and indicators, as symptoms, of factors in the clinical histories of women, but are not especially significant in themselves. Even feminist analyses of post-partum depression treat its emotional manifestations rather more as reactions to, and indicators of, the powerless and conflict-laden situation of women (for example, Oakley, 1980), than as profound and existentially valid experiences of given individuals.

The medical approach to post-natal depression is, of course, understandable as well as necessary from a clinical point of view as the basis for the formulation of therapeutic regimes, the provision of data for epidemiological studies and as the framework for differential diagnosis. Therefore the defining criteria of post-partum depression, as put forward in the professional medical literature, need to be taken into account as a set of bench-marks for our considerations. Currently three types of emotional post-partum disturbance are recognised (Cox, 1986). The "baby-blues" syndrome has timing (3 to 6 days post-partum) as its most reliable marker; the frequency of its occurrence and its limited duration render it "normal" and thus relatively unproblematic. The most severe form of post-partum disturbance, the "puerperal psychosis", may be distinguished by significant morbidity of thought and affect and by delusions, hallucinations and lack of insight. Its incidence is estimated to be between 0.5% and 1.0%. At the less severe end of its spectrum, it shades over into the much more common depressive state, the post-partum or post-natal depression, under which label the psychotic variant is also sometimes subsumed (Dennerstein et al, 1986); as a disease-entity it is ill-defined and for this reason estimates of its prevalence vary from 3.0% to 45.0% (Dennerstein *et al.*, 1986), the difference in these estimates reflecting the variety of diagnostic criteria used in different studies.[34] The main body of our discussion in this chapter is concerned with post-natal depression in this broad sense.

We did not encounter, in our group, depressive manifestations severe enough to be regarded as psychotic and, to our knowledge, no woman out of those we interviewed sought psychiatric help— though a number said that they had experienced periods of mild to severe depression. On the other hand, the experience of "baby blues" was relatively common, though brief and not perceived as particularly debilitating. The "baby blues" often coincided with problems associated with the establishment of lactation, as the earlier discussion of breastfeeding describes. Women frequently spoke of a period soon after birth when they were "a bit weepy", when they felt mildly depressed and emotionally labile: "Ah, a few days after birth, I'd sort of feel really happy, really ecstatic, and then I'd sort of feel really sort of tearful. But it wasn't real depression. I wasn't going crazy or anything" (Helen).

For some, this was not resolved simply with the passage of time. Heather, for example, left the hospital without her baby for a few days:

I was really tired from visitors and after the operation (Caesarean section) which was really painful, I was just exhausted. By the fourth night I was weepy. They also had me feeding her every three hours and expressing (breast milk). When my milk came in I felt really revolting and uncomfortable...The nurses were coming in all day and interfering with the way I was handling the baby. They were very worried about me; I just did not want to see the baby. So I went out of the hospital and left the baby there for three nights and by the

---

34. A recent NSW Government report thus makes a typically vague statement regarding this condition: "15–20% of women are believed to experience a significant degree od post-natal depression" (New South Wales, Ministerial Task Force, 1989).

end of that time I knew I could handle it. I just needed to be alone with (husband).

But for most women, this period of tearfulness was brief and self-limiting; despite the anxieties experienced at this time, the period was unlike the more lasting and more disturbing complex of negative emotions that surfaced, for some women, during the first trimester. It is to the content of these experiences that our attention is directed here.

FACETS OF DEPRESSION

In our account of the phenomena of post-partum depression, we have chosen to be guided by women's own assessment of their feelings and reactions, their own views of the commensurability of their emotions to the reality of their circumstances. We found that women could distinguish readily between ordinary, "normal" negative feelings on the one hand—and, on the other, depressed states for which they could not completely account in terms of the conditions and events that surrounded them. This is not to say that the latter emotional state was necessarily thought of as illness or abnormality; rather, there was a realisation there was something unexplained, unfamiliar and disproportionately painful in their disturbances.

But these disturbances were always about *something*; and, as we have already pointed out, the contents of these disturbances must be considered in themselves, since they point to dimensions of experience which are significant enough in women's lives to be a focus for anxiety and depression. In other words, in attending to the individual's sense of emotional suffering (Lutz, 1985), we choose to analyse the *pathos*, rather than the pathology, of women's experiences. Furthermore, the fact that these experiences are similar for many women suggests that the social context may play a significant part in their distress. The discussion which follows explores a number of major themes in women's accounts of their feelings and reactions—themes which are major in terms of both their importance to the women themselves and the frequency with which they are voiced.

Overcome

I have to get used to this—being a 24-hour a day life-line…in fact, it is for ever, I will never be the same because he (the baby) will always be my concern, as long as I live (Frieda).

The most important thing to me is surviving through it, you know…I personally think that um being a mother is very important and sometimes the importance of it is really overwhelming actually, the responsibility that you've got. And you don't feel like you can catch up to it, sometimes I don't think you can (Helen).

As Oakley (1986a:24) notes "mother's lives are incurably (sic!) affected by their motherhood; in one way or another the child will be a theme for ever". The most dominant and prevalent feeling seems to be one of awe and even dread associated with the realisation that one's life has been irreversibly altered, that one is from this point on forever beholden to another human being who is, moreover, completely helpless and dependent. As interview texts quoted above indicate, some women are overwhelmed by the responsibility which their babies' dependency thrusts upon them, its physical, palpable presence in their lives and its permanent mark on their state of mind. They were not prepared for this crucial experience, either emotionally or practically, before the birth. In this connection, Oakley's (1980) analysis of post-partum emotions, in terms of loss of previous self and way of life, addresses a significant, but limited, aspect of this experience. For it is not only the loss of a past pattern of existence and of the previous self that these women perceive and feel. Even more so, the yawning dark space of the future and the unpredictability of it and of the self within it makes many women anxious and fearful and robs them of confidence.

It could almost be argued that here depression is philosophically realistic, as it might also be in circumstances other than the post-partum. When there is heightened sensitivity, due to a variety

of conditions—hormonal, physiological, personal and environmental—there may be a propensity to feel things more deeply.
Depression then may result partly because there are, in given situations, no intersubjectively meaningful cognitive structures within
which such feelings can be contained and absorbed into a cohesive
experience of one's everyday life. Thus Kerry referred to her experience of depression as "a solid block of feeling bad" and Diana
described it as "being in a brown fog". These metaphors suggest
not only negative emotion but also isolation and alienation from
the rest of life. Of course, personal psychological variables play a
significant part here and interact with social forces in particular
ways. For example, we may note that older *primiparas*, i.e. women
over the age of 35, bring into the post-partum period a different
context of meaning due to a relatively larger body of memories and
influences in their past experience, which may include ambivalence, reactions to past terminations of pregnancy, lasting conflicts
with their own mothers, and so on, and which after the birth may
persist in the subconscious in an active way (Raphael-Leff, 1980).

The modern social context presents us with structures which
are rationalised in principle but which do not necessarily provide
detailed specifications for practices subsumed under them. At the
same time, these structures exert both cognitive and material pressures. In the case of motherhood, specifically, physical and
psychological requirements of infant care are understood to
inform mothering activities. However our culture does not
prescribe either unambiguously or in precise detail actions we can
take to meet these—nor, for that matter, criteria by which we can
judge whether, or to what extent, this has been accomplished.
Here the "quality vs quantity of mothering" argument comes to
mind; it has many variants in relation to "working mothers" and is
debated on many platforms in various media—but always incon-
clusively, however often "studies" are quoted regarding effects on
infants and children of various mothering practices and schedules.
It is not surprising, then, that, in general, evidence suggests that in
industrialised countries women are poorly prepared for the
post-partum and are nervous of their ability to care for their
infants, to protect them, to interpret their range of needs, and to

respond, at the same time, to other family pressures (Michaelson, 1988b).

The pervasive aspects of contemporary social life which bear on this situation have been discussed by Giddens in terms of the "disembedding" of social relations "in the light of combined inputs of knowledge affecting the actions of individuals and groups" (1989:17). Local interactions are penetrated by and shaped in terms of social influences quite distant—in both time and space—from various "expert systems", the trust in which underwrites much social action. However, the multiplicity of these influences and their time/space remoteness render phantasmagoric the experiences on which they impinge. Hence individual difficulties in "getting a grip on" particular situations in a way which can be felt to be immediately substantiated.

Where there are no specific guidelines for practices, there are also no routine and established forms of action within which strong feelings can be meaningfully accommodated. Consequently these feelings are experienced as a threat: "(M)uch like sexual behaviour, members of society share a collective interest in managing individual emotional expression (as)...displays of strong feeling are potentially disruptive—they tear at the social fabric" (Middleton, 1986:122). While medical anthropologists and anthropologically aware medical practitioners argue whether or not post-partum depression occurs across cultures (Cox, 1986; Stern and Kruckman, 1987; Harkness, 1987), it does seem to be the case that in most societies—including "advanced" societies until relatively recently—there are beliefs concerning the vulnerability (physically and emotionally) of the post-partum state which lead to practices characterised by reduction of responsibilities, social contacts and information input for the new mother; for example, the "little tradition" (in Robert Redfield's definition) of "doing the month" (of various prescriptions and proscriptions) for women post-partum (Pillsbury, 1982:120). This reduction in the level of interaction is coupled, in a context of relative social isolation, with the continuous presence of the mother's female kin, offering her emotional support and practical help. Indeed, one of the women in our study experienced mild depression precisely when such kinship support was withdrawn:

> I first got weepy about the third or fourth day. And then my mother came down and my husband's family were all down, all staying here, and after all that there was just a real emptiness and I think that was when I started to go down. He was about four months old. I went through a real sort of weepy time then (Denise).

Where comprehensive and intimate interpersonal support is available, it is possible that strong negative emotions are not engendered; on the other hand, should they surface, it might be easier to deal with them amongst women confined in a special and private atmosphere, than it would be under "normal" circumstances. In our culture, following childbirth women are returned to "normal" circumstances, though their emotional and psychological—as well as practical—needs may require special conditions. Quite apart from their concerns with various aspects of infant care, postpartum women may have a number of other worries: about their bodies—the repair of Caesarean or episiotomy scars, weight loss or gain, breast discomfort etc; and about loss of libido and the relationship with partners/husbands. In addition, there is an expectation, based on the cultural representations of pregnancy, that being pregnant is aberrant and that women will postpartum "revert" to normalcy (Breen, 1975:89). Their inability to do this in a way which is satisfactory to them may add to their vulnerability at this time. In such a context, it can be expected that strong emotions sometimes come to the fore and, having done so in a "normal" environment, are perceived as "abnormal". Thus a mother, recounting the depression of friend, commented: "She is three years older than I am but she is very young in the head, and I keep telling myself that she is the hysterical type...but there is always the nagging doubt, you know, that you will (get depressed too)" (Jennie).

The ideas and images supplied by our contemporary culture are pluralistic and contingent, relevant mostly to specific social groups and contexts. In the realm of ideas and values relating to motherhood and family life, recent research in Australia (Richards, L., 1985) has shown this to be the case—though older, "traditional", previously assumed universal and dominant "ideologies" (Wearing, 1984) persist in individuals' awareness without necessarily influencing their behaviour. An unified, cohesive frame of reference that may support, or at least meaningfully structure, the experience of an individual entrapped for a time in her own singular situation (her own time, place and way of "having a child"), is not readily available in contemporary society. Instead, the congruence we have now is contained in the fit between, on the one hand, the fragmentation and professionalisation of support networks and, on the other, the pluralism of beliefs and values across both different social groups and different areas of social life. There is little in such a situation to support anyone who is facing a truly existential moment in her life.

Food, glorious food

The realisation of the impact of a new infant on one's whole life provides the key to the depression that some women feel. But the everyday practical aspects of the care of a baby, particularly when the baby is fretful or unpredictable, constitutes a constant source of stress. We have already indicated (in Chapter 5) that feeding the baby is always problematic. This factor is very clearly emphasised in some of the popular literature on postpartum depression (Welburn, 1980; Dix, 1986) and is here taken up again, now as the second major theme in our present discussion. All depressed women we interviewed showed obsessive and, to an "objective" outsider, excessive concern with feeding and anxiety over both the amount and the pattern of baby's intake. From an emotional standpoint, however, this is understandable, since feeding is literally a question of life and death for the infant and therefore an inescapable responsibility for the mother (especially if she is breastfeeding, as most of the women we interviewed did). Some women expressed anxiety concerning feeding in terms of the very physical dependency of their infant upon them: "sometimes I wonder whether I'm just a big bosom for him" (Helen); and a letter to the editor of NMAA newsletter recounts: "I have lost count of the number of times I have sat out on the back porch at 3 am after yet another feed, in tears, wishing I had a detachable breast which could be lent to my husband (or anyone for that matter) so I could have a break" (Nursing Mothers' Association of Australia, 1985:14).

Because of the fundamental importance of feeding, every aspect of it becomes significant and can, therefore, become a source of anxiety:

> I really got shell-shocked when the sisters at the clinic, one lot were telling me to put her on a complement... and another lot were telling me there was no need for that. And then we'd have another one tell me something else. I got quite frazzled after a couple of weeks (Pam).

> I try to demand-feed, but I just can't tell if it's working...every little cry means trouble. I am completely drained, emotionally and physically... it is all so confusing (Stella).

In a world where eating is routinely an infinitely calculable activity along sundry dimensions of price, amount, weight, calorie value, nutrient make-up, recipe constitution, timing of meals etc., the necessarily uncertain business of baby feeds is disorienting in its absence of boundaries. Danger, and consequently anxiety and even despair, can therefore lurk in the shadows of the vagueness which increases, rather than diminishes, with the proliferation of publications on the philosophies and practices of infant care. Other sources of information are equally unhelpful. We have already shown that professional advice on feeding often bewilders and confuses the new mother, largely due to contradictions which emerge from its many quarters. Despite this confusion—or perhaps because of it—a dependency is created. This in turn is fostered by our culture's emphasis on the importance of "expert" advice and the pressure towards demonstrable manageability of situations and tasks. The institutions of health care have responded to this pressure at various levels with the result that, in the area of childbirth and infant care, a wealth of human experience has been transformed into a set of "problems".

"Problems" in our culture require "solutions"; but where "problems" consist of situations that cannot be defined precisely, the effectiveness of solutions to such "problems" is difficult to demonstrate. Thus the tasks cannot be accomplished nor the dependency needs assuaged for the mother who is anxious and depressed and seeks, therefore, identifiable boundaries for her unease and reliable aid in dealing with its source. Quite often, for example, a depressed and worried mother wants to give up breast-feeding as the bottle is "easier to manage" and "I can actually see how much he has had"—but then the regret and the guilt emerge, which, in turn, need further resolution; and so on: "It took weeks before I could offer his bottle without crying, and it still distresses me to watch other mothers nursing their babies" (Nursing Mothers' Association of Australia, 1985:15).

In many societies, sanctioned routine practices and rituals operate to ensure that appropriate (as distinct from effective) actions are observed. Consequently outcomes do not have to be measured nor, indeed, conceptualised as such. In industrialised societies such as Australia, we have little choice but to try and evaluate outcomes in order to assess the appropriateness of actions, since actions are rationalised according to the nature of the task (or "problem") towards which they are directed. Even activities that are deemed "natural", such as demand feeding, have a rationale put forward by its proponents in terms of its benefits for mother and child and its superior efficiency as a method. It is hardly surprising, therefore, that new and inexperienced mothers become increasingly anxious and depressed as they continue to seek validation of their actions in a situation which, by its very nature, does not lend itself to unambiguous assessment.

All Through The Night

The theme of baby's crying is closely—though not invariably—related to feeding and is subject to the same preoccupations by the depressed (and other) mothers. There are, however, two additional factors related to crying, especially prolonged, excessive crying. One is the difficulty for the mother of determining the reason for the baby's distress and resolving it (thus ensuring that the crying stops); the other is lack of sleep to which a mother with a fretful infant may be subject. The need to manage the situation is very prominent with both. Mothers are generally unwilling to let the baby cry—although in the past women did leave babies to "exercise their lungs"—and instead employ a variety of techniques such as rocking, singing, carrying the baby in a back or front pack, burping and patting, taking it for rides in the pram or car, playing tapes of "womb-sounds", using baths, dummies and hammocks, placing a clock by its crib, and so on. The options sometimes read as endless and suggest the desperation that many parents feel in the face of irritable or inconsolable babies.

The uncertainty that lies behind these strategies—the inability of a parent to determine why a baby is crying and what to do to stop it—is a main cause of anxiety:

> I found that I was going through a lot of highs and lows, particularly lows because she was a very crying baby. She was very unsettled at that stage...You reach that stage of total despair—especially the crying got to me, I couldn't cope with that...sometimes you don't see anything you can do and you're left in a no-man's land...I was a bit weepy...I just felt lost—I didn't know how to cope or how to improve the situation. I look back now and wonder how I got through it (Vanessa).

The infant's cry is a constant reminder, as well as a symbol, of the irrevocable change that has taken place in women's (and couples') lives and of the emotional impact of that change: "Our lives have changed no matter how much you keep on with doing things... I know Tom (husband) was stunned, because he stayed at home for the first five weeks, he couldn't lie down and just have a read because as soon as he would...she'd start crying, or something...I was exhausted and pretty stunned by the whole thing" (Pam).

Lack of sleep has a very tangible effect in terms of fatigue, irritability and loss of concentration. These feelings and sensations in themselves become sources of concern for the mother who is already anxious. Mothers often begin to worry about their own state of mind which, in turn, compounds their anxieties about the baby; indeed, they may overestimate the extent and significance of their infant's crying when they are in a vulnerable and disturbed emotional state themselves. There is also a belief that tense, anxious mothers have tense, crying, "colicky" babies as the tension is conveyed from mother to child by sometimes uncertain and inappropriate responses to daily events as well as through bodily contact ("the way you hold him", as suggested to one of our respondents by her Baby Health Centre sister). This may be so. Nevertheless, in our study we saw women who very clearly became anxious and depressed after their babies took to excessive crying or after feeding difficulties had developed, which women read as evidence of their failure to mother well. With its implications of the distress on the part of the baby and the consequences of lack of sleep for the mother, crying is, we believe, an important if not major cause of anxiety and some depression. A recent Australian study bears this out: difficulty of infants' temperament, including excessive crying, is related to womens' experience of stress post-natally (Terry, 1991).[35]

Almost all first-time mothers experience difficulties with feeding and crying and most are troubled to a lesser or greater extent as they seek to make sense out of the behaviour of their infants. Very few have Natasha's confidence: "With me (looking after the baby) is almost instinct. I think this is because I've had so many nieces and nephews...I'm happy being a mother".

Most mothers need and try to get their babies into a predictable and manageable routine which represents the perceived "normal pattern" of baby behaviour (hence the role of nursing homes for new mothers). Most women also believe that this will come "naturally" or through the use of manoeuvres such as timing of the daily bath, walks, rides in the car and so on. Lack of previous experience

---

35. Terry's paper contains references to a number of U.K. and U.S. studies regarding the relationship between crying and parental stress during early parenting.

with babies, however, which is usual in this society for new mothers, makes the process of comprehending and responding to baby's behaviour problematic. In this situation, instructional literature and "expert" advice may be poor substitutes for spontaneously and slowly accumulated implicit understanding which develops in everyday naturalistic settings—as Natasha's excerpt above suggests—and which may not need to produce, or be dependent on, explicit comprehension of "what is going on". Such comprehension, however, is eagerly sought by contemporary mothers who live their whole lives in settings structured by rationalised accounts of processes and procedures. The search for comprehension is based on the belief in the existence of a "normal" infant behaviour pattern that can provide realistic bench-marks for one's own actions. But like many typifications of the modern life-world (Berger *et al.*, 1974), the "normal" baby is mythic rather than real.

There are historical circumstances, possibly specific to Australia, which may have played a part in the formation of contemporary attitudes in this respect. Deacon (1986) has argued that, under the influence of "Taylorism", the Infant Welfare Movement early this century introduced concepts of "efficiency" and "expertise" into infant care and advocated education and surveillance of mothers, so that children would develop into healthy adults and worthy citizens. As Reiger (1985) pointed out, this approach ignored social determinants of development and health and rendered mothers solely responsible, in both senses of that word. For example, one of the outcomes of the National Conference on Infant Mortality in 1906 was described (Lewis, 1980) as consensus of opinion that maternal ignorance was the fundamental cause of infant deaths. The consequent emphasis on maternal education deprived women of confidence in their community and skills and engendered a need to rely on professionals for instruction in proper methods of infant care.

Looking Back, Feeling Guilty

I did not feel the bond of motherhood the way I thought it should feel. I suppose there was a resentment in there. Many a time I wonder why we had had her! I know this sounds awful, but it is honest (Alison).

Sometimes guilt has different sources:

Oh (a good mother is) just somebody who has more energy (than me) or was stronger or was... changed his nappy more often and managed to get the washing done and kept the house clean or something...That was my major battle really, sort of battling against this...I thought sometimes people thought that I wasn't doing very much, simply because I was at home looking after the baby, that I was having an easy time and that I was a bit slack (Helen).

As we have discussed in the previous chapter, many women are concerned about bonding and expect this to be a distinct and special experience. In the present context it is necessary to emphasise again the anxieties women have about the relationship with the baby if bonding is perceived to have been impaired by circumstances surrounding the birth and early postpartum. Difficulties with feeding and crying are then often explained in terms of bonding failure and blame is extended both to self and to the conditions seen to precipitate the problem. The ensuing guilt and anxiety may linger for months and compound the psychological and physical burdens of early motherhood.

Many women also feel guilty and anxious about being tired, irritable, unloving and miserable in a situation where positive emotions are expected and where, as Marshall points out, the idealisation (the "ultimate fulfilment account") of motherhood denies "that mothers may have negative feelings or reactions" (Marshall, 1991:72). Negative feelings are generally unacceptable in our society and especially so if no socially valid reasons can be proffered for them—and even then (e.g. in grief) their duration is expected to be limited and their manifestations contained. New mothers, of course, are expected to be fulfilled and happy, joyful even. For those who feel the opposite—who feel tense, angry, resentful, frightened, trapped or simply overwhelmingly sad—their emotions are a source of puzzlement and shame.

The lack of moral and practical support for new mothers may exacerbate these feelings; the current absence of such support stands in sharp contrast to the prominent public discourse in recent years on the status and significance of motherhood and birthing. While many books, magazines and pamphlets about mothering emphasise the joyfulness of this process and provide resources for the management of possible problems of new motherhood, few women have an extended family or a circle of close friends and neighbours who will help with housework chores, cook a meal, wash nappies, show excitement about the new baby, work through perceptions and feelings as they arise for the new mother, and in general be around to interpret daily events and integrate the new mother and her infant into the life-world. "It is really good being interviewed", one mother said to us, "at least I know you really are interested in all the little details that everyone else finds boring".

THE BURDEN OF CHOICE

The relative social isolation of the new mother is not helped by the apparent freedom of choice that the contemporary woman has with respect to various mothering practices. It is now largely a question of personal choice whether to breast feed or not, demand feed or not, keep the baby by or in the bed or in its own room, return to work or stay at home, insist on shared parenting or not, and so on. Ideological forces work to champion some of these apparent choices, but there are enough options presented popularly for most women to feel that the decision-making is theirs and that they will not be judged for choosing in particular ways.

While there are obvious advantages in the liberalism that emphasises personal freedom over fixed patterns of behaviour, women must now necessarily wade through a vast repository of information that appears relevant to their decision-making in terms of the physical and psychological welfare of the infant, the wider family, and the woman herself. Few women have access to all the skills to enable them to evaluate such information efficiently, and many are confused in their efforts to do so by the latest "true story", resulting from the study most recently published and publicised. Furthermore the freedom—and therefore, realistically, the imperative—of choice and the wealth of information and expert opinion on various aspects of infant care signal effective lack of support by the social order as they demonstrate a normative void with respect to the *practices* of motherhood, in a context of meaning where the achievement of its *state* is nevertheless explicitly valued.

Consistent with these conditions, as we have found in our research, is the lack of emphasis on attention to mothers once they have given birth. Pregnancy and labour are subject to concentrated attention and effort, but new mothers must elicit support. The difficulties that they experience subsequent to delivery (and the immediate period thereafter) are regarded as routine, ordinary, minor and trivial contingencies of life "in the normal course of events". It is incumbent on the women themselves to resolve these problems and to "cope" (Crouch and Manderson, 1987b). Usually this is exactly what women do; they cope alone in face of countless miseries, worries and disorientation, fatigue and loneliness, personally having to solicit support from partners, relatives, friends, and social agencies when their needs are greatest and their emotional and physical resources maximally taxed.

RELATIONSHIP MATTERS

The thoughts and feelings which preoccupy women postpartum are focused on themselves in relation to their babies. There are other problems too—changes in the relationship with a partner, changes in household finances with often a shift to one income, sexual difficulties—but these were all of secondary importance to the women with whom we worked. We noted, like Pertot (1981) did, that some women did experience a decline in libido, and that this sometimes caused tension between the new mother and her partner. However, most women were likely to deal with this in common-sense terms, as a temporary and normal state that would be resolved in time and would not threaten the basis of the partnership. This contrasted with women's concerns over their relationship with their infants, which was always problematic, open to questioning, examination and assessment. Further, women tended to relate their lack of interest in sex back to issues of mothering. This fits with Kayner and Zagar's findings (1985), from a survey of 121 breastfeeding women, that 62% reported reduced or no desire while lactating. A respondent wrote to us along similar lines: "We discussed our experiences of breast-feeding and the effects on our sexuality. All of us in a group of around twenty were relieved, surprised, pleased, amazed to discover that our experience was so similar, that is, an incredible lack of interest in sex while breastfeeding...to receive the support of the group was fantastic".

In our interviews, the relationship with the partner did not have the same prominence or depth of feeling attached to it as did the dynamics of the interchange between the infant and the mother and the emotions of the mother herself (although admittedly, this is partly because women's feelings and perceptions in relation to motherhood have been the explicit focus of our research). This is not to suggest that women regarded their partnerships as unimportant after the arrival of their child—but it is clear that women's intellectual and emotional as well as physical resources centred around their babies. Some women did report tension that derived from their lack of interest in sex, or the lack of time to spend with their partners, or their lack of interest in talking to their partners about much other than the new baby. Even in addressing these shifts and strains on partnerships, women often returned to the issue of their baby and their relationship with it: "It (the marriage) has been totally different since the baby's been born. We don't spend nearly as much time discussing things; I would be exhausted by seven or eight. With breastfeeding I though I could catch up on sleep during the day, but I'm not the kind of person who can sleep then and so without any sleep it doesn't improve your disposition. I don't think the baby brings us any closer" (Vanessa).

In addition, women tended to talk about their relationship with their husbands in terms of their perceptions of their husbands' attitude towards the baby, so that adult communication was mediated through the infant and sex replaced by parenting:

> I just didn't want sex actually, I don't know why …it's still hard now, though I suppose getting the baby out of the room might help …It's okay, because he (husband) is really involved in the baby too, in a way, I mean, he really likes him and so um…we sort of transferred all our, those sort of feelings onto these nice feelings of just having a baby there, we both really enjoy it so it doesn't matter much (Helen).

And again (though not without problems):

> You don't have much time for each other. But then I see how much he (my husband) loves the baby and that really pleases me, it makes us into a little family. I'm just too tired most nights…Physically our relationship has changed from what it was. And we never argued before the baby was born but we started to have arguments after he was born. It's not what I expected (Beverly).

A number of women experiencing problems with feeding, crying and depression were puzzled and disturbed by their husbands' "turning off" or incomprehension of their difficulties. As Diana, for example, relates, "I lie in bed awake wondering what he thinks…am I being judged? We never talk about it—does he know how I feel?" And Janet is concerned about her husband's jealousy of the baby: "When I was pregnant, I was still the same person…but now, everything is different…and I am different, Sam (husband) complains…the baby takes so much out of me; I think he is upset because I don't baby him any more".

In many cases however, the changes within the partnership were perceived as extremely positive:

> Ever since I was pregnant little things worried me and we talked them out, he's become more honest with me and I think that

honesty will keep going and the fact that we can be more honest with each other will make a lot of difference, it's just made us more sensitive towards each other (Jennie).

We often say, "What did we ever do without him?", you know, it just seems so much of our life now...he is very easy and we've just had that sort of relationship where we don't argue, it's very platonic as well and although at times when I've been tired I'd get crankier than I'd ever been and things like that...he'd try to understand. I suppose that could really affect a marriage if it wasn't handled properly. But I think in a lot of ways relationships are deepened and you're more aware of people...I suppose it just completely changes your outlook on life (Denise).

WHO CARES?

We have given attention in the discussion above to the social and cultural context of early motherhood as a background for the anxiety and depression that some women experience during this period. In so doing, we are not arguing against the importance of hormonal, personality or dispositional factors of depression. We recognise that such factors may well be involved and compound the effects of social circumstances. On the other hand, any interventions will occur in the social realm primarily, and for this reason we need to be explicit about the ways in which the social organisation of early motherhood places women in jeopardy. An aspect of that context is the way in which "those professions who have assumed this responsibility (of caring for motherhood) have re-worked the notion of caring beyond all recognition, so that technical services in the pursuit of physical, quantifiable ends are overwhelmingly what 'caring' for motherhood has come to mean" (Oakley, 1986c:143). The structure of services for mother and child emphasises surveillance, not caring. Thus, although there are problems in defining postpartum depression, the professional literature favours assessment of patients, screening to identify cases (or "at risk" women) and appropriate therapy in terms of differential diagnosis (Cox, 1986; George, 1987).

It is certainly the case that some women do become sufficiently disturbed and dysfunctional during the postpartum to need structured intervention, sometimes including effective pharmacological measures. But for every woman who becomes a "patient" clinically, there are many others suffering similarly and battling on as best they can without help, and others suffering less but still experiencing practical difficulties, anxiety, stress and depression to varying degrees. These women may perceive that their "condition" is akin to illness, or may be seen as such, and so feel ashamed and reluctant to seek help (in Australia, depression has typically been regarded by non-sufferers as a sign of weakness, an inability to "pull oneself together"). Other women may be fobbed off when they seek help, as may happen when sources of advice are fragmented and geared to dealing with "cases" and "problems" rather than to caring for people and their daily concerns. Focus on technicalities of baby care from a clinic sister, a prescription rather than time to talk about the baby's colic from a family doctor, a blandly reassuring pep-talk by a counsellor—such acts of inattention may discourage and damage many women in need of help.

This will continue, we suggest, while the implicit view persists that postpartum depression, in keeping with its definitions as a "disease" or "disorder", is a condition that affects some identifiable category of "at risk" women. But we might also see such depression as a condition of the state of early motherhood, variously distributed amongst individuals at any time. In other words, all women are "at risk", although only some might become depressed and very few seriously so. The suffering experienced by women during early motherhood under modern social conditions is manifested in various ways: as clinical depression in some, and as confusion, fatigue, anxiety, irritability and lack of confidence in many others. The pressures and anxieties of early motherhood tend to recede with time, but few women get through early mothering without some insecurity, uncertainty, sleepless nights, or resentment. Though, of course, these feelings are experienced by different women in different ways, they represent a general dimension of women's existence. This dimension, in turn, can be conceptualised as an integral aspect of a total social pattern within which its constituent elements arise.

Such a view implies that practical assistance needs to be available to all new mothers. At present, there is some support, but the extent to which women are able to take advantage of it largely reflects their own social position: their willingness to call on others in the community and to seek friendship and practical assistance without feeling patronised, their ability to pay for other kinds of help (housekeeping, nappy wash services, and so on) and the confidence to question the advice offered by the health services in order to clarify certain issues. Poor women, those with limited education, or with poor English language skills, are least likely to challenge the views of a doctor or nursing sister, join the NMAA, or lobby for childcare. Even so, community organisations are an essential component in responding to the needs of new mothers.[36] The effectiveness of social care has been demonstrated in the case of new mothers (Oakley, 1986c) as well as in the area of general health (Berkman, 1984). Given that ideally such help should be available to all new mothers and not be dependent on a "diagnosis" of postpartum depression, it is possible to think of it as a preventive measure which operates at the interface of welfare services and health care. There is no rejection of the value of medical treatment in this suggestion. In fact, we hold that a juxtaposition of the "medical model" with a more "holistic" or social model of health care implies a false dichotomy which is ultimately harmful.

Oakley (1986c) rejects the usefulness of the dissemination of information concerning postpartum depression on the grounds that such information can lead to the increased medicalisation of a range of feelings and experiences which have a social cause. Both

---

36. There has, in fact, been a growing interest in postnatal depression in the popular press from the early 1980s, demonstrating a greater public acceptance of, and interest in, this subject. To a lesser extent, there has also been a parallel trend to establish new, or enlarge existing, services for new mothers, as evidenced, for example, in New South Wales by organised attempts to bring together interested parties and individuals into a community network (Social Impacts, 1987).

Welburn (1980) and Cox (1986), on the other hand, have lamented the lack of information about postpartum depression and the poor treatment that depressed new mothers receive as a result. While apparently contradicting each other, these two positions both fail to take count of the complexity of postpartum depression or, in our extended formulation, of the postpartum condition, with the combination of physical, personal, social and cultural factors which make this period such a difficult and precarious time in a woman's life. As Harkness (1987:208) has put it, "The inner experience of pregnancy and the postpartum period reflects biological functioning as well as individual history and life-circumstances, all within the context of cultural practice and meaning shared by mothers giving birth and those that attend them". Perhaps, then, the information that needs to be disseminated concerns the nexus between emotional well-being and given social contexts. Widespread understanding concerning this connection may, in time, act as a catalyst for social changes that will improve the situation of all women in recognisably vulnerable situations.

In this chapter, we have explored the main dimensions of women's experience during the postpartum and, in turn, related these dimension to prevailing conditions and collective meaning systems of contemporary society. This mode of analysis will be pursued further in the following chapter, in which we attempt to review and integrate our discussion of the transition to motherhood, its phases and aspects and the individual experiences and social circumstances involved in it.

PART FOUR
AFTERTHOUGHTS

Chapter 7

PEOPLE MATTER, IN THEORY

The findings of our research can be summarised at a very general level in the following propositions: firstly, contemporary collective representations of maternity and particularly birth centre around the ideological emphasis on the concept of the "natural"; and secondly, there exists, at the same time considerable diversity of women's practices, reactions, responses, feelings, attitudes and opinions concerning birth and the circumstances of early motherhood. This diversity is nonetheless patterned, the patterning being predominantly in terms of motifs and themes—and their interrelationships—rather than in clusters or types of persons acting in particular ways. Most of these motifs and themes have been analysed in previous chapters. In this chapter we shall attempt to analyse this patterned diversity per se and to explore its meaning in the context of the processes and the spirit of contemporary social life.

IT TAKES ALL KINDS

We have already pointed out that presently, in comparison with the post-WWII years (as well as before that), new mothers are more heterogeneous with respect to age, marital status, occupation and sexuality. As sociologists we can assume that this variability may be linked, in some systematic fashion, to the diversity, as noted above, of cognitive, emotional and practical processes involved in the transition to motherhood. Yet there is no evidence in our findings for direct correspondences between specific structural and cultural patterns as, in general, particular perceptions and attitudes do not consistently characterise given age, status or other groupings of individuals. In any case, for our mode of analysis, it is more important to take note of the pluralism in both the structural and cultural dimensions than to seek an ordered relationship between them. The pluralism itself can then be conceptualised as a manifestation, in the realm of individuals' private sexual and reproductive conduct, of the "post-industrial", "post-modern" character of contemporary social life, often described as "dispersed", "anarchic", "indeterminate" (for example, Rose, 1991), based on multifarious consumption which is "firmly established as the focus, and the playground, for individual freedom" (Bauman, 1989:46) and fuelled by the production of signs and images that have become commodities in their own right (Baudrillard, 1981). We need to examine in some detail the sense in which the term "pluralism" has been used here, before the connection between this "pluralism" in reproductive practices and "the condition of postmodernity" (Harvey, 1989) can be discussed further.

Pluralism is not chaos.[37] Some configurations can be detected in the varied contents of our material. There is, for example, a discernible patterning of women embarking on motherhood. We have identified a number of types: single, mostly low-income, young mothers (under 21), the mid-twenties married women (usually having worked for a few years "until the children arrive"), single women around thirty (sometimes with no definite career), married women in their early thirties (normally with an established career or work history) and the 35+ "older mothers" (mostly married and often with high professional or occupational status). These are overlapping and internally somewhat mixed categories. Nevertheless, it might be expected that these categories

---

37. No reference to Chaos Theory is intended.

could suggest links between structural factors and allegiance to various cultural norms, beliefs and practices. Since, however, our research has not been carried out in the methodological framework of a sample survey, but rather with thematic analysis as its main aim (as discussed in Chapter 1), we have not attempted to establish such connections in any quantitative sense. This is not merely an *a priori* methodological decision; the nature of our material also suggests strongly that attempts to order our data in terms of direct correspondences between structural and cultural/attitudinal categories will be severely thwarted by the obstinately individualistic accounts of our informants' experiences.

Thus any connections which a survey-type study in this area could have made between "face-sheet variables" on the one hand, and "responses" on the other, may have obscured a number of important factors in the experiences of women which, individualistic though they may be, we need to comprehend in order to understand fully the nature of the impact of social forces on persons and their practices. More importantly, perhaps, comprehension at this level is necessary to inform our hunches about the manner in which individual actions become absorbed by the dynamics of change in social processes.[38]

OLDER MUMS, FOR INSTANCE

Most new mothers in their mid- to late twenties have assumed that they would have a child within a few years of marriage: "it is just something you do—all part of the course" (Elaine). This group of our respondents, then, could be said to represent the "standard" pattern of family formation where childbearing is taken for granted and occurs within a relatively narrow time-span of a relationship.

---

38. This is, of course, one of the most vexing problems in social theory. If our work makes any contribution towards its clarification, it will be in our attempt to link the question of 'structure/agency' with data from a specific area of social life where, fortuitously, change proceeded at an fast and therefore observable pace (see footnote 43. below).

Nevertheless, there is often great diversity in the specific circumstances of the timing of the first pregnancy:

> We were going to have children—but this one came a year too early.
> It wasn't planned...we were using the rhythm method. We were
> using it half-heartedly. I must have timed it wrong. (When I found
> out) I cried—it came as a bit of a shock. I think I was more scared
> than anything else of having another miscarriage. As time went by I
> got more anxious about it, more pleased and happy about it
> (Natasha).

> We were young when we got married, so we thought we'd have the
> first three or four years together to sort out the marriage and to get
> a house... last October I came off the Pill and four months later I
> was pregnant (Cheryl).

> My periods went skew-whiff for a while, so I went off the Pill. I
> thought, if I fell pregnant, O.K., but didn't really think about it. I
> fell pregnant one month later—I was really surprised! Anyway, for
> the first few months, I was overcareful, really (Pamela).

Despite considerable differences in detail among them, these
extracts suggest a pattern of actions which, in general, allows
conception to occur on the tacit assumption that it is part of the
expected course of events, presently already under way. Not all
women embark on motherhood within this frame of mind,
however. Against the background of the "standard" pattern exem-
plified above, there are apparently deviant trends, often differenti-
ated in quite specific terms. Let us take the example of "delayed
motherhood":

> I was forty and so if I was going to have a child—I'd have to do it.
> Really just deciding that it was an experience I did not want to miss
> out on—I wasn't really feeling maternal (Angela).

> Well it was really a case of then or never, and I had got to the stage
> when I thought that if I didn't have one then, I'd never have one,
> and I suppose throughout my life...in the cases where I was in a
> relationship where I could have had a child, for one reason or

another like work or something like that...I'd always put it off...But it really was something that I did not want not to have done (Pam).

During the period when our research was being carried out, a Sydney newspaper article (Rodell, 1985) referred to women like Angela and Pam as the "late bloomers". The article was entitled "The last chance baby boom" in reference to the rise in first-time births amongst older women—the term "older" being employed in this connection since 30 is the average age at which medical texts suggest a woman falls into the category of an "elderly" or "older primigravida" (Garrey, 1978; Llewellyn-Jones, 1982).[39] The article proposes that "a generation (of women) raised on feminism has gone to University, taken its place in the professions, married perhaps, built careers. Some having reached their 30s have heard the biological clock ticking away" (Rodell, 1985:17). This generalisation fitted the common-sense understanding of the broad social trends of the day and the concerns women over 30 were therefore likely to have in relation to motherhood, given the implications of advancing years for the physical and social demands of parenting. Thus the article presented a composite portrait of a middle-class, well-educated professional "liberated" (as a young adult in the 70s) woman who had invested time and energy in the advancement of her career and was finally, in the nick of time so to speak, making a bid "to have it all".

Most of our informants in this age-group could, in general, answer to this description in terms of their level of education and socio-economic status. However, our data suggest that it is not possible to extrapolate from this complex of variables to attitudes, motives and emotions of women in this group. Marie's case illustrates this point well. At the time of our interviews, she was 43 and had been married for 18 years. A university degree had qualified her for a responsible and well-paid position; her husband was a successful businessman. But, in contrast to the stereotype, Marie saw herself as a working woman rather than a career woman and

---

39.   There is general agreement in professional literature that obstetric performance declines slowly from about 25 onwards and that risks of pregnancy increase appreciably after the age of 35.

her relationship with her husband was relatively old-fashioned in terms of both the domestic division of labour and attitudes to marriage. In Marie's case, there was no great conflict between motherhood and work; she was willing to compromise the former for the sake of the latter. It was her husband who feared that a baby would represent "the infusion of a disruptive element into the peaceful life of our household". An unhappy and frustrating childhood had apparently made him wary of family life and he was unwilling to risk changes in a satisfactory and predictable pattern of life that was lodged in a secure relationship, good income and shared interests and activities.

A week after the birth of her daughter by Caesarian section, Marie talked quietly but with assurance about her reproductive history. Some years into the marriage, she had begun thinking— and eventually talking—about having children, without, however, any positive response from her husband. Marie then stopped taking the Pill following a "unilateral decision" on her part. Before pregnancy finally occurred, there had been a prolonged difficult period in the marriage, with sulking on the husband's part and anxiety due to ambivalence in expectations for Marie. She was now delighted about the baby, though still uncertain about her husband's attitude, although "he has been very good, really" since the birth. In a subsequent interview three-and-a-half months after the birth, however, she said:

> He (the husband) used to lecture me all the time during the pregnancy ...not to fret too much over the child...or to spend too much time...I used to worry about this a bit—though, as things have turned out, I should have gone by my knowledge of the person rather than his words, since he now appeared to be a totally devoted and even somewhat over-concerned parent himself.

Marie planned to return to work after the maximum amount of maternity leave (one year after the birth of the child). Her contentment with the present situation came as a bit of a surprise: "I am not lonely or bored or any of the things I thought might happen away from work, deprived of adult company". Marie saw her planned resumption of work more as an attempt to restore the couple's previous ordered existence than as the return to her own professional life.[40]

We may profitably compare this account with Diana's story. When her daughter was born, Diana, then 39, had been successful for some time in a competitive field where one "has to maintain the momentum" at all cost. She resumed work two weeks after she came home from the maternity hospital. For the first few weeks she worked mainly at home but soon added two days a week at the office. At this point she said: "You need another environment and the input from it—also the discipline: to get ready and get out of that door". But the situation was not free of conflict because there is the old predicament:

> I am torn in some ways. I like the things I do, but I would also like to stay here (home) and play mummies and do all that—but bearing in mind what I know about myself, the compromise solution appeared to be best.

Four months later, things were no easier:

> This is a difficult time. There is too much work, I am splitting myself too many ways…(in all this time) I have not been able to have a week with nothing else to do but to be just domestic…(but) I am a perfectionist; I like to see things done properly and it is irritating to see my standards slipping.

Clearly Diana was not quite comfortable within herself: "Am I a silly goose for not being entirely devoted to my career? Other mothers work full time, they take it in their stride and don't feel they're missing out on the baby…both situations (baby and job) are a matter of total commitment, so how can they be reconciled?"

In contrast with Marie, Diana had had a number of serious relationships before her marriage of 6 years' standing. The decision to

---

40. At the time of writing, Marie has been out of the workforce for a few years; she returned to her old job when her daughter was one year old, but resigned 12 months later, as both she and her husband preferred her to be a "full-time mum".

have a child was the result of perceiving that "it was clear that (this) relationship was going to work out. I could not keep the relationship childless and I could not wait any longer". Diana's husband felt children to be necessary for a marriage; he probably also had definite feelings about appropriate maternal behaviour, since Diana now had "a sense of being judged by him". However, "maybe this is in my own head—there may be an expectation to be judged". There was also the uncertainty about the issue of another child. "Will I condemn him to be the father of one? It is hard to separate what I think about it from what I think I ought to think about it".

Like Marie, Diana had her baby by Caesarian section; but it was the slightly older and somewhat more conservative Marie to whom this was a considerable disappointment as she was looking forward to a "completely natural" birth. Certainly a glib generalisation which might categorise both Diana and Marie as "economically independent, liberated and aware modern women" would gloss over this and all the other important differences between them. The complexities of their respective situations are patterned in quite specific ways with different significant factors in each one. At the same time, Marie and Diana act in unison, structurally speaking, as they both participate in the social matrix which has brought forth the prominence of "older" motherhood. This is not merely a question of superficial similarities in terms of their social positions. At a more fundamental level, despite the obvious differences between them in terms of personal circumstances, attitudes and feelings, both Marie's and Diana's lives are equally enmeshed with the social dynamics of their time in quite determinate ways.

For example, a little more than coincidence of factors such as age and socio-economic status, the services of a specialist obstetrician and private hospital accommodation, might have been involved in both women's Caesarian deliveries. We suggest that general conditions of quite a different kind have a role here. It is possible that many older women contemplate childbirth (or younger women put it off) partly because they know that current obstetric practice contains various options for manipulative labour management and relief of pain, including, if necessary, Caesarian delivery. To say this is not to defend the high rates, in recent times, of surgical interventions in labour (*Sydney Morning Herald* 30 April 1990:17, and 1 May 1990:18)[41] but to make the point that their availability "when necessary" (however questionable the definition of the limits of this term may be) and their relative safety, constitute part of the common-sense knowledge about childbirth that forms the background to women's decisions regarding reproduction. (Naturally the use of reliable contraception is understood as the necessary condition for such decisions to be effective[42]). It is simply easier to put off childbearing for yet another year or two, if one knows that labour is nevertheless likely to be relatively safe and free from gross trauma.

We are not equating this knowledge with personal attitudes and preferences that actually favour intervention in labour. For example, Susan, 32 and a nurse by profession, stated before her labour most adamantly that she did not "want to be cut" under any circumstances. In the event, she struggled valiantly for 24 hours with contractions which were painful and exhausting, but not sufficiently effective; finally, she gave in to a Caesarian delivery. Later, she told us of her disappointment, but she added "in the old days the baby would have remained stuck and both of us would have died". The very fact that Susan was set against a Caesarian delivery before her labour started, showed that she nevertheless acknowledged it as a realistic option in principle.

In Diana's case, there was agreement, without much anxiety, with her obstetrician's recommendation for an elective Caesarian delivery. She even "looked forward to it as a challenge, in a way".

---

41. This information relates to Caesarian sections in undertaken by specialists and to their patients in private hospital accommodation.

42. This matter is raised here only to point out that, in the discussion so far, it has been appropriate to take the role of contraception for granted as the awareness of its availability and widespread use are by now incorporated in the common-sense stock of social knowledge. It may have been easy, therefore, to overlook the fact that this knowledge is an important aspect of the social dynamic which unifies, at the collective level, women's individualistic decisions and actions.

Marie, on the other hand, was looking forward to a natural birth and felt let down by the turn of events; nevertheless, as, in the course of her labour, "there quickly came the point when I would have done anything to ease the pain", the obstetrician's decision to perform a Caesarian section (because of foetal distress) came as a relief. Similarly, freedom from pain was definitely the most important consideration for Frieda, 38 when her son was born by Caesarian section. Frieda acknowledged that she had always been abnormally afraid of childbirth. She was therefore very happy to settle for an elective Caesarian: "if there were to be problems (in labour), I would not know about them and would not suffer". In Frieda's case, it was partly this fear which had led to delayed motherhood; she had avoided conception until her mid-thirties, the full-term pregnancy following two miscarriages two years apart.

PERSONS OR TRENDS?

This discussion is not advocating or defending Caesarian deliveries. Rather, it serves to illustrate a more general point: that diverse, individualistic choices are made in the context of social conditions which intertwine with individual action in ways that channel the socially visible corpus of these personal moves into what can be identified as "trends" in collective terms. Clearly in given situations individual women appraise conditions—or information available to them about these conditions—in relation to their own specific circumstances and motivations (including those that may have a subconscious basis). Choices from a limited number of realistically possible options are made on the basis of such appraisals. In this sense personal behaviour can be socially generative as individuals' assessment of circumstances leads to overtly similar actions that coalesce into components of social life at the structural level (Crouch, 1981).[43] Thus the trend towards delayed childbirth can be connected meaningfully with a number of operative factors in contemporary society—but at the same time, these factors cannot all be expected to account equally for the actions of individual women whose collective conduct actually constitutes the trend. We can elaborate on this point through a discussion of the relationship between delayed motherhood and work in the contrasting cases of Diana and Marie.

The increasing involvement of women in the work-force, especially in its more prestigous segments, is the result largely of both a liberalisation of attitudes towards, and changes in conditions affecting, the occupation of women—notwithstanding resistances and constraints barring or disabling, in various ways, such involvement. At the same time, these circumstances have also brought about considerable pressures, especially on middle-class, well-educated women, to work and achieve recognition, status and a good income. These pressures are at least partly constituted by women's perceptions, many of which are responses to subtle normative messages from the cultural milieu that confabulates the "success ethic" of capitalism with the assertiveness of the women's movement and the "self-actualisation" popular philosophy of modern individualism (Lasch, 1985). But they also result from economic constraints or from employment opportunities to which women have learned to become increasingly sensitive, often through activities of others already pursuing a career. Most importantly, these pressures also result from women's interests and

---

43. Much of contemporary social theory deals with this question of the relationship between structure and agency (for example, Giddens, 1984 and 1989; Bauman, 1989). We have eschewed extensive reference to this debate in order to keep the main thread of our discussion close to our material and its main themes. However, we have tried to avoid a mere gloss of fundamental theoretical questions by attempting to link our interpretations of the data with specific aspects of general conceptual issues, in a way which may enhance the understanding not only of our material, but also of the relevant theoretical points. This is not as presumptious as it sounds, since often discussions of the structure/agency issue in the literature specifically devoted to it are quite abstract and rarely test the capacity of their formulations to chart in detail specific areas of social life.

inclinations and women's desire to translate them into action in a socially recognised manner. The more internalised the goals, the more powerful the pressures—which need to be reconciled, in turn, with the actual, as well as the perceived, demands of motherhood.

Diana quite clearly experienced this situation as a conflict. Part of the reason for the conflict was Diana's lack of an explicitly political position—she was not a feminist—to provide an impersonal rationale and external reference point for her actions, which were therefore experienced as reactive, rather than proactive. The conflict was there, of course, before the birth of the child; it was what had kept Diana childless for six years of her marriage. But her genuine love for her work and her ambitions in relation to it were perceived in opposition to motherhood only when the baby was actually there, inciting inescapable practical and emotional responses.

By contrast, the social *milieu* had a more coherent effect on Marie. Her work had made it socially acceptable to be childless—as well as, subsequently, to become an "older mother". At this point she was not sufficiently committed to her career to experience great internal conflict between her professional role and her mothering (though perhaps some of the potential for conflict along those lines was "syphoned off" by her husband's attitude and the need to reach a compromise with him). Thus Marie's occupational status actually saved her from social eccentricity in relation to childbearing (both before and after the birth), almost ironically through the mediation of the very same cultural factors that occasioned Diana a great deal of pain. Ironically again, it is at the same time, fair enough to say—sociologically—that both women are contributors to the same social trend.

The changing directions of social pressures and expectations have interacted in similarly diverse ways with activities of women in other new mothers' groupings we have identified. For example, the young single mothers of to-day are not under the same pressure to have their babies adopted as was the case in the 50s and 60s. This coincides with the greater social acceptability of all forms of sexual expression and the attrition in the importance of the traditional concept of marriage as a prerequisite for parenthood. The provision of financial support by the State for single parents officially underwrites these social changes and, at the same time, materially facilitates any decisions to keep the baby. But single motherhood cannot be *explained*, in a causal sense, by these conditions at the level of individual action; for this, knowledge of the particular circumstances of each case is always necessary.

Some young women, for example, become pregnant accidentally and subsequently perceive that "having a child" gives them some definable status which is, at least temporarily, preferable to unemployment or an unskilled job. This seems to have been the case with Rose (quoted in Chapter 6) who felt, on balance, that the baby enhanced her beach-oriented mode of living even though he (the baby) curtailed to a large extent the actual activities involved. Stella, on the other hand, embarked on motherhood as part and parcel of a whole "alternative" philosophy of life, as a most significant component of her own personal growth and an opportunity to bond even more strongly, through the process of home birthing, with friends who shared her point of view. (In the event, a difficult labour that ended in a hospital delivery and a bout of depression after the birth led to Stella's taking refuge with her parents, after which we lost touch with her.) In the comparison between Stella and Rose, we again see how very different individual cases may, on certain criteria, be identified as belonging to a specific category or constituting a particular social trend. It is tempting to speculate that this happens at the popular, common-sense level in the contemporary social context because this context is culturally diverse and normatively uncertain, thus producing, with its smorgasbord of values and options, the need to formulate "trends" and classify individuals in order that social reality be made comprehensible and the lifeworld manageable.

MOTHERHOOD IS A SENTENCE, NOT A WORD

The discussion in previous chapters has already shown that within this complexity the attainment of motherhood and, particularly,

its place and timing for individuals, appear almost uniformly
contingent and problematic for women, albeit to varying degrees
for particular persons. This fact points to the great significance of
motherhood for the identity of contemporary women—a *significance* more profound than that of two or three decades ago (while
the *importance* of motherhood in relation to women's social status
has diminished since). Before effective contraceptive usage, the
major transition in a woman's life was marriage, since this led, as
a matter of course, to a number of fundamental changes. But
during the recent decades, increasingly the first pregnancy, rather
than marriage, came to be the most significant "rite of passage".
The transition to motherhood now represents a change of state
and a different phase of being, whereas other changes—such as
marriage, for example—are often no more than alterations in the
context of activities which themselves remain relatively similar.
This statement is not merely a distillation of some our interview
material, one of its "common themes". It also expresses an assessment of circumstances at the level of social organisation and
cultural imagery.

The contemporary "companionate marriage" (or "relationship") shades more and more explicitly into a combination of
sexuality, friendship and the sharing of activities between relatively
autonomous social equals who are partners in an alliance of individualism within the confines of one of the very few remaining,
apparently still resilient, established social institutions—the
private household (Holton, 1987). At the same time, more and
more women participate in the workforce—or in some other
non-domestic pursuit, such as study or community/committee
work—and are therefore recognised as individuals according to
their positions in the world of public structures and affairs. Under
these conditions, matrimony (or cohabitation) adds a new dimension—"the most significant other" (Berger and Berger,
1983:180)—to women's lives without, however, altering them
profoundly in respect to either most everyday practices or the
process of self-definition which is now expected to envelop
"worked upon" relationships (Giddens, 1989). Maternity,
however, changes both; furthermore, it is an emotional and

material tie for which there is no dissolution by decree or mutual consent. A mother is permanently branded and the more voluntaristic and singular a woman's entry into the condition of motherhood, the greater the significance of its mark she bears.

WHO PAINTS THE PICTURE?

In this view, the myth of the "good birth" and the ideology of the "natural" labour and "bonding" are cultural symbols of the meaning and import of motherhood for contemporary women. Our research has shown that all women are cognisant of these myths and many hold them sacred[44] in principle, even though their actual childbearing practices may be quite eclectic. This disjunction between concepts and action, or practice and image, may be a common characteristic of the human condition and has been recognised in social science since at least the classic work of Le Play (referred to in Bottomore, 1987) at the individual level, and Durkheim (1964) from the supra-individual, *sui generis*, perspective. But in recent times more attention has been given to social representations in their own right, to the way in which these are collectively "constructed" and to the manner in which entrenched interests (in particular, those of capitalism and patriarchy) dominate "social discourse", thus influencing—and often directing—activities and attitudes at both collective and individual levels. Little emphasis is given, generally, to discrepancies between dominant, "hegemonic" ideas and the variety of patterns of social action. When discrepancies are recognised, they are interpreted as challenges or resistance to the dominant model (e.g. Hall and Jefferson, 1976) or, in relation to the "ideology of motherhood" (Wearing, 1984; see also Fraser, 1987).

There are, of course, such challenges. But, more importantly, it has to be noted that the discrepancies between representations and actions occur even where the ideological model is apparently generally accepted as both valid and valuable. It seems therefore

---

44. In the sense of Durkheim's (1961) distinction between the sacred and the profane.

that the existence of the ideology is important in itself, quite apart
from its functions as either a model for individual action or, alter-
natively, as an object of social contestation. In fact, part of our
argument has been to show that cultural images of birth are primarily proclamations rather than icons; their ideological dimension
depends crucially on their prior symbolic meaning. We may say
that such images operate as modern mythologies expressing, for
safe keeping, so to speak, our concepts of universal truths and our
deepest aspirations and fears in *illo tempore*, the primeval time
beyond the flow of everyday reality (Eliade, 1960). In the instance
of birth, the quintessential *incipit vita nova* archetype,[45] this is
located in the eternal realm of the "natural". But what are the
origins of the specific depictions within such mythologies?

Discussions of "hegemony" or dominant ideas and images
"socially constructed through discourse" generally take place in a
context where these ideas are deemed reactionary and oppressive,
associated as they are with the interests of some elite, ruling or
dominant class or category of persons—in the case of reproduction, for example, the "male-stream" (O'Brien, 1981). But the
presently prevailing childbirth model does not appear to serve any
dominant interests in the established sense. The ideological clashes
concerning birth procedures characteristic of the 1970s and early
1980s had by the late 1980s resulted in a situation where the oppo-
nents of the then dominant "medical model" of birth have successfully moulded what has in fact now become the prevailing,
"natural", "mother-centred", imagery of the day—however
common medical management of labour may still be in practice,
and however sovereign remains the position of doctors within the
system of health-care professions. It seems that the influential
"trendy" segment of the middle class, and especially its newly
socially competent and confident female members, have been the
dynamic agents in this victory of radical *chic* over established

---

45.   Eliade (1960: 28) holds that, obscure though mythical themes are in
modern society, they survive nevertheless, especially so in relation to entirely
new beginnings, for example, New Year, birth of a child, moving into a new
house, etc.

medical orthodoxy. This demonstrates, firstly, the inappropriate-ness, in the present instance at least, of common assumptions concerning inevitable overlaps between the interests—and posi-tions—of the bourgeoisie and extant holders of social power; and secondly, the complex, multi-dimensional nature of the relation-ships between gender, sources of social power and ideology. The complexity defies the notion of the union of "dominant interests" and "androcentric" thought, often imputed as a general character-istic of contemporary culture (for example Thiele, 1986).

An alternative theoretical account is perhaps more appropriate: the situation we have described above may be an example of the efficacy of "post-industrial" social players (Touraine, 1984) who have had the capacity, the sense of timing and the means to influ-ence the projection of favoured ideas and images onto the public arena. In contemporary "post-modern" culture which "swims, even wallows, in the fragmentary" and is characterised by "ephemerality, discontinuity and chaotic change" (Harvey, 1989:44), domination may occur at many levels, being lodged in the control of the process of change in knowledge (Touraine, 1984) and, particularly, in the induction of the course of that process, rather than in the suppression or regulation of its mani-festations. Thus social knowledge is increasingly fragmented in its basic parameters as values and beliefs of "post-modernity" become more and more "plural, local and immanent" (Fraser and Nicholson, 1988) and individuals conduct is bound by "tempo-rary contracts" valid only for some "language games" that consti-tute the social system (Lyotard, 1984). Therefore different social groupings—different assemblages of "players"—become dominant in different areas of social life and "seduction replaces repression as the dominant form of control" (Platt, 1989:662).

But once seduction becomes an important factor, the possibility of pleasure from various options may become a criterion for indi-vidual choice, diffusing, in turn, the mobilising impetus of commitment to some offerings in our contemporary marketplace of ideas and practices. This seems to have happened with the "natural" birth paradigm even though it can be argued that it has represented a social movement, to an extent, since some of the actions under its umbrella have challenged or broken "the system of social relations" (Melucci, 1989:38) to a considerable degree. As Chapters 3 and 4 have shown, the concept of the "natural" has strong moral connotations which pull powerfully at the strings of the guilty and puritan hearts that are still hidden, we suggest, in contemporary individuals' pleasure-seeking bodies. It may thus be that the appeal to nature is a "symbolic mediation" (Melucci, 1989:48) of the process of individualisation, which is said to be one of the motives for participation in collective action in contemporary society. Then it is tempting to deliberate about the applicability of the term "collective action" to women who follow, to a greater or lesser extent, the natural birth paradigm (i.e. to ask: do they act "together", or do they act, *as it happens*, "the same"?) and to try to decide whether one can label these actions a "social movement"—and, should this label be chosen, whether its various connotations enhance our understanding of the phenomena under consideration.

In this regard, we propose a more descriptive formulation in our attempt to "scale the slippery slope" (Tilly, 1985) between individual and collective levels of action. It simply seems to be the case that some of the ideas associated with the natural model have captured the imagination of the public at large as they apparently relate to major preoccupations and conflicts of contemporary individuals, particularly women. At the same time, in practice, individual activities are necessarily realised in a pattern of multiple interdependencies of social relations and personal considerations which include those of pleasure and the avoidance of undue effort and stress in both material and psychological terms—the "comfort principle" (Bauman, 1989) of the life-world of post-modernity. Seduction as a mode of control therefore works differentially, rather than directionally.

INSECURELY FRAMED

These considerations extend somewhat our analysis of the social significance of birth imagery in previous chapters. As we have already argued, images of birth are social metaphors projecting meanings that relate to significant aspects of the culture. But our culture now is characterised by a dispersion of a previously (relatively) unified system of beliefs and values—or, to paraphrase some current sociological formulations, by a fragmentation of the previously "totalising" social narratives (Lyotard, 1984)—and therefore those meanings do not all emanate from centralised sources; as well, they do not necessarily reach all social actors—and those within their target range may be affected by them in different ways.

Contemporary cultural images, then, are neither as focused as the erstwhile traditional, normatively oriented metaphors, nor as securely anchored in legitimate knowledge as the subsequent emancipated and "progressive" (i.e. "modern") models of scientifically rationalised action. By contrast, the plasticity and instability of contemporary images enables, perhaps even fosters, deviations from them in actual behaviour. It is quite possible that "post-modern" images are held and attitudes maintained (for a time) precisely because their forms are open to a degree of interpretation *in performance*. Paradoxically, too, their fuzzy edges make them adhere quite firmly at the most general level of social representation as, for example, with the idea of the "natural" which appears to derive seductive power from its lack of precise definition and its consequently broad—if questionable—denotative field.[46] As Bauman (1989:47) suggests, post-modern consumerism envelops not only products and commodities, but also experiences that meet "the needs of self-construction". Since those needs are emancipated from objective sources and limits, the ways in which they can be met are most likely to be conceived in very

---

46.   Of course, we are not implying here that the concept of the "natural" represents some kind of "grand narrative" with universal normative applications, but merely that it is central to a number of beliefs and practices in a particular "interpretative communty" (Harvey, 1989).

general terms. Hence the possibility that a need can be met by a variety of means; hence also doubt that satisfation has been attained.

Though "needs of self-construction" are reified and thus enmeshed with other, more objectively referenced, needs, the subjective criteria by which they are judged make the effective public negotiation of them difficult—even though, in the case of childbirth, as with many other "needs of self-construction", the formulations of the needs themselves (e.g. for autonomy and fully conscious experience in labour) have emerged out of public debates in various forms. Public negotiation is possible, of course, in political terms, when vested interests dispute the defining terms of certain needs. This does not always happen in established institutionalised ways. According to Nancy Fraser, such negotiations take place in the arena of "the social" which is "a site of discourse about people's needs, specifically about those needs which have broken out of the domestic and/or official-economic spheres that earlier contained them as 'private matters'. Thus, the social is a site of discourse about problematical needs, needs which have come to exceed the...domestic and economic institutions of male-dominated, capitalist society...(it is) a space in which rival interpretations of people's needs are played out" (Fraser, 1987:101).[47]

Quite so; the above description fits the case of the childbirth dispute very well. Rival interpretations of "people's needs" (or, rather, of their *agent-provocateurs*) might be winners or losers in this arena of public discourse concerning erstwhile private matters, where problematical needs of women in labour might

---

47.   Obviously Fraser uses "site" and "space" metaphorically; but the concept of "the social" therefore lacks proper definition since its "site" or "space" are identified in purely relational terms, i.e. by the contestations which take place within them. We have quoted this passage because it describes concisely the class of contestations to which the natural birth debate belongs. However, given that the nature of these contestations has been specified, "the social" itself becomes superfluous. The use of the term in this chapter has been purely heuristic, with the above qualification borne in mind.

have justifiably been flagged and championed. But as the debate fed back into the consciousness and experience of persons in the reflexive manner typical of contemporary society (Giddens, 1989), the new public conceptualisations of the old private matters became, individually, private problems—not necessarily, in every case, to be ameliorated, but certainly always to be solved, one way or another.

In overview, then, traditional birthing and post-natal practices were linked to religious and moral precepts, the emancipation from which resulted, after a time, in the modern, scientific, rational approach to labour that centred around the safety of the foetus. In both cases the authoritative underpinnings for practices were visible and unambiguously located and the criteria for standards of performance were objective: with the traditional model, the observance of procedures as laid down; and in the modern medical model, the "good outcome". Such relatively unequivocal statements cannot be made about the more recent situation. Here the authority is dispersed and the criteria are experiential and subjective; the onus is on persons, and mostly on the woman herself, to judge both the observance of procedures and their success in terms of her performance and her feelings and, indeed, her pleasure. The evaluative notion of "success" has not lost strength as the result of attrition in socially objectified criteria of performance. On the contrary—perhaps precisely because of this attrition—it is a public, universally recognised "orienting principle" (Markus, 1987) which, in relation to birth, painfully intrudes into women's intimate experiences and private lives. Consequently the evaluation is fully realised only in the subjective context of internal conflict and continuous reinterpretation of experience.

INTERNAL QUESTIONS

The personal, private realm where the "orienting principle" finally hits home occupies the interstices of the life-world that are left vacant after the institutionalised components of individuals' lives have been parcelled out according to the requirements of the various structures of working life, social life, community life, leisure activities etc. Paralleling the way in which the schism between the private and public spheres is lodged within, rather than between, persons (as discussed in Chapter 3), these lacunae are contested by competing claims from the free market in values and meanings which constantly integrate the "system" with the "life-world" (Soper, 1990) in the arena of "the social" (Fraser, 1987). The individuals of the audience in the arena's vast amphi-theatre are differentially affected by the display; they process their reactions and make their choices in various ways.

It is questionable whether the liberty this implies constitutes freedom, if freedom is defined as being part of a meaningful life when it is absent from it as a problem (Zijderveld, 1974). This absence is, of course, from the internal life, since an unselfcon-scious individual with a concrete, meaningful and situated exist-ence may still actively pursue social freedom for self and others. The subject of contemporary society and culture, with her "de-centred identity" (Lash and Urru, quoted in Harvey, 1989), may engage in such pursuits, but she does so predominantly in order to resolve inner tension—i.e. to gain freedom from them— as her activities are directed, in the main, to sundry private and personal "problem areas" from which these tensions are seen to arise.

The last section of this chapter shows that our discussion has rebounded—not with the circularity of an empty argument, but inside the hermeneutic dynamic which returns an inquiry to its starting point, altered and re-defined in the process. We commenced our research with an investigation of women's experi-ences, organised them around significant themes and, in turn, analysed these in the light of recent social changes. This has brought us back to a consideration of individuals' experiences— this time understood as constitutive elements of contemporary social life, their very singularity representing one of its systematic aspects.

It would not be productive, we feel, to pursue this analysis further "in terms of" one or another "post-modern" sociological account. For one thing, we would have difficulties in deciding whether to refer to some variant of post-modern sociology or—a different matter altogether (Featherstone, 1988)—to a particular account of post-modernity. The decision would be further hampered by the fact that, within each of these alternatives, a large number of theoretical options appears to be available. We do, of course, have preferences for some, rather than others, of these options. But in the present discussion, doing justice to our material has been our prime consideration. In relation to this task, the current theoretical approaches do not make readily available conceptual tools with which to carve out this material into an appropriately intricate yet meaningful object—though there is no shortage of "models" to employ in the construction of sundry versions of the object's general shape, should one wish to do so. Contemporary social theories, in most cases, rest on concepts the systematic referents of which cannot easily be brought down to the level of individuals' activities in everyday life. Therefore we have pieced together our account mainly in our own data-grounded and inspired terms, using eclectically (just like our informants, in relation to their birth and parenting practices) sensitising concepts from various sources, where these have offered clarification or support.

Put differently, commonsense prevailed in the end, as it did, mostly, for the women with whom we worked. At this point we should recall Pamela's story which opened our discussion of women's experiences in Chapter 3. It is now pertinent to observe that Pamela gives an impression of being relatively free from the need to construct her actions in a particular way. She does what she can under given conditions in terms of what she perceives, variously, as appropriate for different aspects of the task at hand. Many women in our group acted in the same way, though some were internally somewhat constrained by their need for a meta-theory of conduct. We empathise with the sense of unease produced by this need and yet we also appreciate the eclectic accommodation to circumstances which is necessarily made to render the job possible, since an analogous quandary is contained in our own work.

This analogy is neither superficial nor rhetorical. Instead, it refers to an epistemological stance based on the assumption that every one of us—everybody, in fact—has a direct knowing relationship with the world. Human knowledge of the world is partial in both senses of that word, but it is realistic nonetheless, not primarily because the "truth" of its contents can be "tested" or "proven" somehow, but because all our action is knowledge-able as we go about our business constantly having hunches and formulating propositions, in both thought and deed, about the states of affairs that contain and confront us. Theoretical activity is no exception—and neither is everyday practice. Our discussion has continually combined the two, merging both objective and intimate knowledge and experience of our informants with our theoretical, as well as personal, understandings. The result may be somewhat untidy, but, significantly for us, it leaves visible the varied dynamics of its human and conceptual sources. It also allows most our questions to remain open; for all of us involved in this discussion, this is as it ought to be.

REFERENCES

Ackroyd, S. and Hughes, J. A. (1981) *Data Collection in Context*. London: Longman.

Adams, J. L. (1983) The use of obstetrical procedures in the care of low risk women. *Women and Health*, **8**, (1), 25–34.

Albury, W. R. (in press) The positivistic outlook and medicine. In *A Social History of the Bio-medical Sciences* (5 vols), M. Piatelli-Palmarini (ed.), vol.1, 3. Milano: F. M. Ricci.

Allan (no family name provided) (1985) Birth of Thomas: Allan's Report. *Canberra Home Birth Association Newsletter*, November–December, 30–33.

Anon. (1982) Homebirth: magic, martyrdom—or madness? *Parents and Children Magazine*, **2**, 30–33.

Anon. (1984a) Birth Report. Childbirth Education Association (Australia) *A.C.T. Newsletter*, March/April, 29.

Anon. (1984b) Birth Report. Childbirth Education Association (Australia) *A.C.T. Newsletter*, November/December, 9.

Arms, S. (1975) *Immaculate Deception*. New York: Bantam Books.

Arney, W. R. (1980) Maternal-infant bonding: The politics of falling in love with your child. *Feminist Studies*, **6**, (3), 547–570.

Australia, Bureau of Census and Statistics (1970) *Yearbook of the Commonwealth of Australia*, **56**, Canberra: Commonwealth Bureau of Census and Statistics.

Australia, Department of Immigration and Ethnic Affairs (1984) *Selected Characteristics of the Population of Australia* (Chart). Produced for the International Conference on Population, Mexico City.

Australian Bureau of Statistics (1990) *Births, Australia, 1989*. Canberra: Australian Government Publishing Service.

Balaskas, J. (1983) *Active Birth*. London: Unwin Paperbacks.

Barnes, J. A. (1979) *Who Should Know What? Social Science, Privacy and Ethics*. Harmondsworth: Penguin.

Baudrillard, J. (1981) *For a Critique of the Political Economy of the Sign*. St. Louis: Telos Press.

Bauman, Z. (1989) Sociological responses to post-modernity. *Thesis Eleven*, **23**, 35–63.

Bennett, A. (1986) Degree of intervention in childbirth. Paper presented at a Conference on Birth: A Normal Process? Hazards of Medical Intervention. Centre for Continuing Education, Australian National University, Canberra.

Bennett, A., Hewson, D., Booker, E. and Holliday, S. (1985) Antenatal preparation and labor support in relation to birth outcomes. *Birth*, **12**, (1), 9–16.

Berger, B. and Berger, P. (1984) *The War Over the Family*. Harmondsworth: Penguin.

Berger, P., Luckman, T. and Kellner, H. (1974) *The Homeless Mind*. Harmondsworth: Penguin.

Bergum, V. (1989) *Woman to Mother: A Transformation*. Granby, Mass.: Bergin and Garvey Publishers.

Berkman, L. F. (1984) Assessing the physical health effects of social networks and social support. *Annual Review of Public Health*, **5**, 413–432.

Bertaux, D. and Kohl, M. (1984) The life-story approach: a continental view. *American Review of Sociology*, **10**, 215–37.

Bettelheim, B. (1961) *Symbolic Wounds. Puberty Rites and the Envious Male*. New York: Collier Books.

Bhaskar, R. (1989) *Reclaiming Reality*. New York: Verso.

Blackie, P. (1986) *Becoming a Mother after Thirty*. Oxford: Basil Blackwell.

Block, C. R. and Block, R. (1975) The effect of support of the husband and obstetrician on pain perception and control in childbirth. *Birth and Family Journal*, **2**, 43–50.

Block, C. R., Norr, K. L., Meyering, S., Norr, J. L. and Charles, A. G. (1981) Husband gatekeeping in childbirth. *Family Relations*, **30**, (2), 197–204.

Blossfeld, H. P. and Huinink, J. (1991) Human capital investments or norms of role transition? How women's schooling and career affect the process of family formation. *American Journal of Sociology*, **97**, 1, 143–168.

Bottomore, T. (1987) *Sociology: A Guide to Problems and Literature*. London: Allen and Unwin.

Bowlby, J. (1953) *Child Care and the Growth of Love*. Harmondsworth: Pelican.

Bowlby, J. (1969) *Attachment and Loss*. New York: Basic Books.

Bowley, A. J. (1985) Bonding—obstetric fact or psychological fiction? *Breastfeeding Review*, 7, 13–15.

Breen, D. (1975) *The Birth of a First Child. Towards an Understanding of Femininity*. London: Tavistock.

Brook, D. (1976) *Naturebirth: Preparing for Natural Birth in an Age of Technology*. Harmondsworth: Penguin.

Brown, M., Finlayson, C. and Mayo, H. M. (eds) (1943) *The Australian Mothercraft Book*. Published for the Mothers' and Babies' Health Association of South Australia. Adelaide: Rigby Ltd.

Burns, A. (1983) Population structure and the family. In *The Family in the Modern World*, A. Burns *et al.* (eds), pp. 49–66. Sydney: Allen and Unwin.

Callan, V. J. (1985) *Choices About Children*. Melbourne: Longman Cheshire.

Chirawatkul, S. (1993) *Sood Leod, Sood Look*: Social Construction of Menopause in Northeastern Thailand. Brisbane: Unpublished PhD dissertation, Tropical Health Program, University of Queensland.

Clarke, J. (1984) A coward has a home birth. *The National Times,* 1–7 June, 25–26.

Connell, W. R. and Irving, T. H. (1980) *Class Structure in Australian History.* Melbourne: Longman Cheshire.

Corea G. *et al.* (eds) (1987) *Man-made Women: How New Reproductive Technologies Affect Women.* Bloomington, Indiana: Indiana University Press.

Cox, J. L. (1986) *Postnatal Depression.* Edinburgh: Churchill Livingstone.

Crouch, M. (1981) Philosophical realism and social science. Paper presented at 50th ANZAAS Congress, Australian National University, Canberra.

Crouch, M. and Lovric, J. (1989) *Paths to Performance: Gender as a Theme in Professional Music Careers.* Sydney: The Australia Council.

Crouch, M. and Manderson, L. (1987a) Changing images of childbirth. Paper presented at the 56th ANZAAS Congress, Massey University, Palmerston North, N.Z.

Crouch, M. and Manderson, L. (1987b) Keeping afloat: post-partum experience among Australian women. Paper presented at the 1st Conference of the Public Health Association of Australia and New Zealand, Sydney.

Crouch, M. and Manderson, L. (1993) Parturition as social metaphor. *Australian and New Zealand Journal of Sociology,* **29**, (1), 1–18.

Crowe, C. (1985) "Women want it": *In vitro* fertilization and women's motivations for participation. *Women's Studies International Forum,* **8**, (6), 547–552.

De Vries, R. G. (1984) "Humanising" childbirth: The discovery and implementation of bonding theory. *International Journal of Health Services,* **14**, (1), 89–104.

Deacon, D. (1985) Taylorism in the home: the medical profession, the Infant Welfare Movement and the deskilling of women. *Australian and New Zealand Journal of Sociology,* **21**, (2), 161–173.

Dennerstein, L., Varnavides, K. and Burrows, G. (1986) Postpartum depression: a review of recent literature. *Australian Family Physician,* **15**, (11), 1470–1472.

Dick-Read, G. (1942) *Childbirth Without Fear. The Principles and Practice of Natural Childbirth.* London: William Heinemann Medical Books Ltd.

Dick-Read, G. (1950) *Introduction to Motherhood.* London: William Heinemann Medical Books Ltd.

Dick-Read, G. (1955/1966) *Antenatal Illustrated. The natural approach to happy motherhood,* 3rd edn. London: William Heinemann Medical Books Ltd.

Dick-Read, G. (1968) *Childbirth Without Fear,* 5th edn., L. Snaith and A. Coxon (eds) London: Pan Books.

Dix, C. (1986) *The New Mother Syndrome.* London: Allen and Unwin.

Douglas, M. (1966) *Purity and Danger: An Analysis of Concepts of Pollution and Taboo.* London: Routledge and Kegan Paul.

Dowrick, S. (1986) Women take control "naturally". *The Sydney Morning Herald,* September 2, 15.

Drake, E. F. A. (1902) *Maternity without Suffering.* Philadelphia PA: The VIR Publishing Company.

Durkheim, E. (1961) *The Elementary Forms of the Religious Life,* 2nd edn. London: Routledge and Kegan Paul.

Durkheim, E. (1964) *The Division of Labour in Society* (Simpson, G., trans.) New York: Free Press.

Dyer, E. D. (1963) Parenthood as crisis: A re-study. *Marriage and Family Living,* 25, (2), 196–201.

Edgar, D. (1981) Implications of changes in population trends for non-work activities and services. Paper presented at the Conference on Implications of Australia's Population Trends, Department of Immigration and Ethnic Affairs, Canberra.

Ehrenreich, B. and English, D. (1973) *Witches, Midwives and Nurses: A History of Women Healers.* Old Westbury, N.Y.: The Feminist Press.

Eisenstein, H. (1991) *Gender Shock.* Sydney: Allen and Unwin.

Eliade, M. (1960) *Myths, Dreams and Mysteries.* London: Harvill.

Encel, S. (1978) Capitalism, the Middle Class and the Welfare State. In *Essays in the Political Economy of Australian Capitalism,* II, E. L. Wheelwright and K. Buckley (eds), pp. 148–168. Sydney: ANZ Book Company.

Ewy, D. and Ewy, R. (1982) *Preparation for Childbirth. A Lamaze Guide,* 3rd edn. Boulder, Col: Pruett Publishing Co.

Featherstone, M. (1988) In pursuit of the post-modern: an introduction. *Theory, Culture and Society,* 5, (2/3), 195–215.

Finch, J. (1984) "It's great to have someone to talk to": The ethics and politics of interviewing women. In *Social Researching: Politics, Problems, Practice,* C. Bell and H. Roberts (eds), pp. 70–87. London: Routledge and Kegan Paul.

Firestone, S. (1970) *The Dialectic of Sex: The Case for Feminist Revolution.* New York: William Morrow Co.

Frankenberg, R. (1984) Incidence or incidents; political and methodological underpinnings of a health research project in a South Italian town. In *Social Researching: Politics, Problems, Practice,* C. Bell and H. Roberts (eds), pp. 88–103. London: Routledge and Kegan Paul.

Fraser, N. (1987) Women, welfare and the politics of need interpretation. *Thesis Eleven,* 17, 88–106.

Fraser, N. and Nicholson, L. (1988) Social criticism without philosophy: An encounter between feminism and post-modernism. *Theory, Culture and Society,* 5, 373–394.

Friedan, B. (1968) *The Feminine Mystique.* Harmondsworth: Penguin.

Frydman, G. (1987) *Mature-Age Mothers.* Ringwood, Vic.: Penguin.

Galtung, J. (1973) *Theory and Methods of Social Research.* London: George Allen and Unwin.

Garrey, M., Govan, A. D. T., Hodge, C. and Callander, R. (1978) *Gynaecology Illustrated.* Edinburgh: Churchill Livingstone.

Gaskin, I. M. (1985) What to say to a mother during labour. *New Parent,* 7, 2, 6–7.

Gemmell-Smith, P. (1986) The battle with natural birth. *Sydney Morning Herald,* 4 September, 15.

George, T. (1987) Management of psychiatric problems of the puerperium. *Current Therapeutics,* 5, (7), 121–123.

Giddens, A. (1984) *The Constitution of Society.* Cambridge: Polity Press.

Giddens, A. (1989) *The Consequences of Modernity.* Cambridge: Polity Press.

Glaser, B. and Strauss, A. (1967) *The Discovery of Grounded Theory.* Chicago: Aldine.

Golde, P. (1980) *Women in the Field: Anthropological Experiences.* Berkeley: University of California Press.

Goode, W. and Hatt, P. (1952) *Methods in Social Research.* New York: McGraw-Hill.

Greenberg, M. and Morris, N. (1974) Engrossment: The newborn's impact on the father. *American Journal of Orthopsychiatry,* 44, 520–531.

Haire, D. (1973) The Cultural Warping of Childbirth. *Journal of Tropical Paediatrics and Environmental Child Health,* Special Issue, 19, 171–191.

Hall, S. and Jefferson, T. (eds) (1976) *Resistance to Rituals: Youth Subcultures in Post-war Britain.* London: Hutchinson.

Hammersley, M. and Atkinson, P. (1983) *Ethnography: Principles in Practice.* London: Tavistock.

Harding, S. (1984) *The Contradictions and Ambivalences of Feminist Science.* Philosophy Department, University of Delaware (mimeo).

Hardy-Wardrop, F. (1978) Pregnancy and Health. *Blackmore's Nature and Health Journal,* 5, 36–40.

Harkness, L. (1986) *Birth: Where and How.* Sydney: HWW Guides.

Harkness, S. (1987) The cultural mediation of postpartum depression. *Medical Anthropological Quarterly* (New Series), 1, 194–209.

Harper, J. (1980) *Fathers at Home.* Ringwood, Vic.: Penguin.

Harper, J. (1992) From secrecy to surrogacy: Attitudes toward adoption in Australian women's journals 1947–1987. *Australian Journal of Social Issues,* 27, (1), 3–16.

Harper, J. and Richards, L. (1979) *Mothers and Working Mothers.* Ringwood, Vic.: Penguin.

Harvey, D. (1989) *The Condition of Postmodernity.* Oxford: Basil Blackwell.

Haug, F. (1987) *Female Sexualisation.* London: Verso.

Hennenborn, W. and Cogan, R. (1975) The effect of husband participation on reported pain and probability of medication during labor and birth. *Journal of Psychosomatic Research,* 19, 215–222.

Hewson, D., Bennett, A., Holliday, S. and Booker, E. (1985) Childbirth in Sydney teaching hospitals: a study of low-risk primiparous women, *Community Health Studies,* 9, (3), 195–202.

Holton, R. J. (1987) The idea of crisis in modern society. *British Journal of Sociology,* 38, (4), 503–520.

Homans, H. (1982) Pregnancy and birth as rites of passage for two groups of women in Britain. In *Ethnography of Fertility and Birth,* C. MacCormack (ed.), pp. 231–266. New York: Academic Press.

Homebirth Access Sydney (1982) The cultural warping of childbirth, *Newsletter,* 1, 8–9.

Humerick, S.S. (1984) Mastery: The key to childbirth satisfaction. *New Parent,* 6, (1), 10–12.

Illich, I. (1976) *Limits to Medicine.* London: Marion Boyars.

Jones, W. L. (1979) The investigation of counter-predictive research outcomes through the method of analytic induction. In *Counter-predictive Research*

Outcomes, J. A. Martin, (ed.), pp. 18–35, Canberra: Research School of Social Sciences, Australian National University.

Jordan, B. (1978) *Birth in Four Cultures.* Montreal: Eden Press.

Kaplan, E. A. (1992) *Motherhood and Representation. The Mother in Popular Culture and Melodrama.* London: Routledge.

Kaplan, M. M. (1992) *Mothers' Images of Motherhood.* London: Routledge.

Kayner, C. E. and Zagar, J. A. (1985) Breastfeeding and sexual response. *Breastfeeding Review,* **6**, 36–39.

Kerstake, P. (1985) Fathering—The pain, the pride, the privilege. *NMAA Newsletter,* **21**, (7), 8–9.

Kiernan, K. E. (1988) The British family: Contemporary trends and issues. *Journal of Family Issues,* **9**, (3), 298–316.

Kilmartin, L. and Thorns, D. C. (1978) *Cities Unlimited: The Sociology of Urban Development in Australia and New Zealand.* Sydney: Allen and Unwin.

Kirkman, M. and Kirkman, L. (1988) *My Sister's Child.* Ringwood, Vic.: Penguin.

Kitzinger, S. (1962) *The Experience of Childbirth.* London: Gollanz.

Kitzinger, S. (1978) *Women as Mothers.* Glasgow: Fontana.

Kitzinger, S. (1979) *Birth at Home.* New York: Oxford University Press.

Klaus, M. H. and Kennell, J. H. (eds) (1976) *Maternal-Infant Bonding.* St. Louis: C.V. Mosby Co.

Klaus, M. H. and Kennell, J. H. (eds) (1982) *Parent-Infant Bonding.* St. Louis: C.V. Mosby Co.

Klaus, M. H and Kennell, J. H. (1983) Setting the record straight (editorial). *Journal of Pediatrics,* **4**, (102), 575–576.

Klee, L. (1986) Home away from home: the alternative birth center. *Social Science and Medicine,* **23**, (1), 9–16.

Kuhn, T. S. (1970) *The Structure of Scientific Revolution,* 2nd edn. Chicago: Chicago University Press.

Lamaze, F. (1970) *Painless Childbirth: Psychoprophylactic Method* (1st pub. 1958). Chicago: Henry Regnery & Co.

Lamb, M. (1982) Second thoughts on first touch. *Psychology Today,* **16**, (4), 9–11.

Lasch, C. (1985) *The Minimal Self: Psychic Survival in Troubled Times.* London: Picador.

Leach, E. (1976) *Culture and Communication: The Logic by which Symbols are Connected.* Cambridge: Cambridge University Press.

Lees, S. and Senyard, J. (1987) *The 1950s: How Australia became a Modern Society and Everyone got a House and a Car.* Sydney: Hyland House.

Lewis, B. (1984) Birth: What it's really like. *Sydney Morning Herald,* 11 October (Life and Home Supplement), 1–2.

Lewis, B. (1986) *No Children by Choice.* Ringwood, Vic.: Penguin.

Lewis, J. (1980) *The Politics of Motherhood.* London: Croom and Helm.

Llewellyn-Jones, D. (1982) *Fundamentals of Obstetrics and Gynaecology,* 3rd edn. London: Faber and Faber.

Lomas, P. (1966) Ritualistic elements in the management of childbirth. *British Journal of Medical Psychology,* **39**, 209–213.

Lumley, J. (1980) The image of the foetus in the first trimester. *Birth and Family Journal,* **7**, 5–14.

Lumley, J. and Astbury, J. (1980) *Birth Rites, Birth Rights: Childbirth Alternatives for Australian Parents.* Melbourne: Sphere Books.

Lutz, C. (1985) Depression and the translation of emotional worlds. In *Culture and Depression,* A. Kleinmann and B. Good (eds), pp. 63–100. Berkeley: University of California Press.

Lyotard, J.-F. (1984) *The Postmodern Condition.* Minneapolis: University of Minnesota Press.

Macfarlane, A. (1977) *The Psychology of Childbirth.* Cambridge, Mass.: Harvard University Press.

Macintyre, S. (1977) The management of childbirth: A review of sociological research issues. *Social Science and Medicine,* 11, 477–484.

McNeil, M., Varcoe, I. and Yearley, S. (eds) (1990) *The New Reproductive Technologies.* New York: St Martin's Press.

The Macquarie Dictionary. (1982) Sydney: Doubleday.

McRobbie, A. (1982) The politics of feminist research: Between talks, text and action. *Feminist Review,* 12, 46–58.

Magney, A. (1987) *The Sydney Baby Book.* Sydney: HWW Guides.

Manderson, L. (1981) Roasting, smoking and dieting in response to birth: Malay confinement in cross-cultural perspective. *Social Science and Medicine,* 15B, 509–520.

Markus, M. (1987) Women, success and civil society. In *Feminism as Critique,* S. Benhabib and D. Cornell (eds), pp. 96–109. Cambridge: Polity.

Marsh, G. N. (ed.) (1985) *Modern Obstetrics in General Practice.* Oxford: Oxford University Press.

Marshall, H. (1991) The social construction of motherhood: An analysis of childcare and parenting manuals. In *Motherhood: Meanings, Practices and Ideologies,* A. Phoenix, A. Woollett and E. Lloyd (eds), pp. 66–85. London: Sage.

Martin, E. (1987) *The Woman in the Body.* Boston: Beacon Press.

Mathews, J. J. (1984) *Good and Mad Women.* Sydney: George Allen and Unwin.

Mayes, B. T. (1954) *Practical Obstetrics.* Sydney: Angus and Robertson.

Maynard, R. (1986) Beating the new baby blues. *The Australian Women's Weekly,* July, 166.

Melucci, A. (1989) *Nomads of the Present.* London: Hutchison.

Melzack, R. (1984) The myth of painless childbirth. *Pain,* 19, 321–337.

Merton, R. K., Fiske, M. and Kendall, P. L. (1956) *The Focused Interview.* Glencoe N. J.: Free Press.

Michaelson, K. L. (1988a) Introduction. Childbirth in America: A brief history and contemporary issues. In *Childbirth in America. Anthropological Perspectives,* K. L. Michaelson (ed.), pp. 1–32. South Hadley, Mass.: Bergin and Garvey.

Michaelson, K. L. (1988b) Bringing up baby: Expectations and reality in the early postpartum. In *Childbirth in America. Anthropological Perspectives,* K. L. Michaelson (ed.), pp. 252–260. South Hadley, Mass.: Bergin and Garvey.

Michaelson, K. L. and Alvin, B. (1988) Technology and the context of childbirth: A comparison of two hospital settings. In *Childbirth in America. Anthropological Perspectives,* K. L. Michaelson (ed.), pp. 142–152. South Hadley, Mass.: Bergin and Garvey.

Mitchell, J. (1986) Reflections on twenty years of feminism. In *What is Feminism?*, J. Mitchell and A. Oakley (eds), pp. 34–48. Oxford: Basil Blackwell.

Mitford, J. (1992) *The American Way of Birth*. New York: Dutton.

Moncrief, A. and Evan, P. (1953) *Diseases of Children*, 5th edn. London: Edward Arnold & Co.

Montagu, A. (1967) *Life Before Birth*. London: New English Library.

Mullins, P. (1988) Is Australian urbanisation different? In *A Sociology of Australian Society*, J. M. Najman and J. S. Western (eds), pp. 517–541. Melbourne: Macmillan.

Mutrym, C. A. (1985) The psychological impact of caesarians. *New Parent*, 7, (1), 2–32.

Navarro, V. (1976) *Medicine Under Capitalism*. New York: Prodist.

Nelson, W. E., Vaughan, V. C., McKay, J. and Behrman, R. E. (eds) (1979) *Textbook of Pediatrics*. Philadelphia: W. B. Saunders and Company.

New South Wales, Department of Public Health (1965) *Obstetric Practice in NSW*. Sydney: Division of Maternal and Baby Welfare.

New South Wales, Ministerial Task Force on Obstetric Services in New South Wales (1989) *Maternity Services in New South Wales: Final Report*. Sydney: NSW Department of Health.

Nicholson, J. (1983) *The Heartache of Motherhood*. Ringwood, Vic.: Penguin.

Nilsson, L. (1965) *A Child is Born*. New York: Delacourte.

NMAA (Nursing Mothers' Association of Australia) (1985) *Newsletter*, July/August, 14.

Nobel, E. (1985) Beyond natural childbirth. *New Idea*, 3 August, 95–109.

Oakley, A. (1975) Wisewoman and medicine man; changes in the management of childbirth. In *The Rights and Wrongs of Women*, J. Mitchell and A. Oakley (eds), pp. 17–58. Harmondsworth: Penguin.

Oakley, A. (1979) *Becoming a Mother*. Oxford: Martin Robertson.

Oakley, A. (1980) *Women Confined: Towards a Sociology of Childbirth*. Oxford: Martin Robertson.

Oakley, A. (1981) Interviewing women: A contradiction in terms. In *Doing Feminist Research*, H. Roberts (ed.), pp. 30–61. London: Routledge and Kegan Paul.

Oakley, A. (1986a) *From Here to Maternity. Becoming a Mother*. Penguin: Harmondsworth.

Oakley, A. (1986b) *The Captive Womb*. Oxford: Basil Blackwell.

Oakley, A. (1986c) Feminism, motherhood and medicine: who cares? In *What is Feminism?*, J. Mitchell and A. Oakley (eds), pp.127–150. New York: Pantheon.

Oakley, A. (1987) From walking wombs to test-tube babies. In *Reproductive Technologies. Gender, Motherhood and Medicine*, M. Stanworth (ed.), pp. 36–56. Minneapolis: University of Minnesota Press.

Oakley, A., McPherson, A. and Roberts, H. (1984) *Miscarriage*. London: Fontana.

O'Brien, M. (1981) *The Politics of Reproduction*. Boston: Routledge and Kegan Paul.

Olssen, E. (1981) Truby King and the Plunket Society: An analysis of a prescriptive ideology. *New Zealand Journal of History*, 15, 3–23.

Paige, K. E. and Paige, J. M. (1981) *The Politics of Reproductive Ritual*. Berkeley: The University of California Press.

Palkovitz, R. (1985) Father's birth attendance, early contact, and extended contact with their newborns: A critical review. *Child Development*, **56**, 392–406.

Parent's Book Collective (1986) *Feeling Our Way: Experiences of Pregnancy, Birth and Early Parenting*. Ringwood, Vic: Penguin.

Parents and Children Magazine (1986) Focus on fathers: how men turn into dads, **30**, 2.

Pertot, S. (1981) Postpartum loss of sexual desire and enjoyment. *Australian Journal of Psychology*, **33**, (1), 11–18.

Pettigrew, J. (1981) Reminiscences of fieldwork among the Sikhs. In *Doing Feminist Research*, H. Roberts (ed.), pp. 62–82. London: Routledge and Kegan Paul.

Phillips, C. R. and Anzalone, J. T. (1978) *Fathering: Participation in Labour and Birth*. St Louis: C.V.Mosby Co.

Pilgrim, J. (1984a) Unexpected outcomes in the birth experience. In *The Birth Revolution*, W. Whitton (ed.), pp. 16–26. Leura, NSW: Second Back Row Press.

Pilgrim, J. (1984b) Overcoming the effects of an unhappy birth experience. In *The Birth Revolution*, W. Whitton (ed.), pp. 27–37. Leura, NSW: Second Back Row Press.

Pillsbury, B. (1982) "Doing the month": Confinement and convalescence of Chinese women after childbirth. In *Anthropology of Human Birth*, M. A.Kay (ed.), pp.119–146. Philadelphia: F.A.Davis Company.

Platt, R. (1989) Reflexivity, recursion and social life: elements for a post-modern sociology. *The Sociological Review*, **37**, (4), 636–667.

Pregnancy, Birth and the Next Six Months (1987) Sydney: Depin Pty Ltd.

Quinn, N. (1982) "Commitment" in American marriage: A cultural analysis. *American Ethnologist*, **9**, (4), 775–198.

Radcliffe Richards, J. (1982) *The Sceptical Feminist*. Harmondsworth: Penguin.

Rae, J. M. (1961) More comfort needed in maternity wards. *The Australian Women's Weekly*, March 1, 47.

Raphael-Leff, J. (1980) Psychotherapy for pregnant women. In *Psychological Aspects of Pregnancy, Birth and Bonding*, B. Blum (ed.), pp.174–205. New York: Human Sciences Press.

Rapp, R. (1988a) Chromosomes and communication: The discourse of genetic counseling. *Medical Anthropology Quarterly*, **2**,(2), 143–157.

Rapp, R. (1988b) The power of "positive" diagnosis: Medical and maternal discourses on amniocentesis. In *Childbirth in America. Anthropological Perspectives*, K. L. Michaelson (ed.), pp. 103–116. South Hadley, Mass.: Bergin and Garvey.

Reiger, K. (1985) *The Disenchantment of the Home: Modernising the Australian Family 1880–1940*. Melbourne: Oxford University Press.

Reiger, K. (1986) Mothering deskilled? Australian childbearing and the "experts" *Community Health Studies*, **10**, (1), 39–46.

Rice, M. (1984) The advent of Alexander was a family affair. *Sydney Morning Herald*, March 3, 17.

Rich, A. (1976) *Of Woman Born.* New York: Bantam Books.

Richards, L. (1985) *Having Families,* rev. edn. Ringwood, Vic.: Penguin.

Richards, M. R. M. (1985) Bonding babies. *Archives of Disease in Childhood,* **60,** 293–294.

Richman, J. (1982) Men's experience of pregnancy and childbirth. In *The Father Figure,* L. McKee and M. O'Brien (eds), pp. 89–103. London: Tavistock.

Richman, J. (1987) *Medicine and Health.* London: Longman.

Richman, J. and Goldthorp, W. O. (1978) Fatherhood, the social construction of pregnancy and birth. In *The Place of Birth,* S. Kitzinger and J. A. Davis (eds), pp. 157–173. Oxford: Oxford University Press.

Riessman, C. K. (1989) Women and medicalisation: a new perspective. In *Perspectives in Medical Sociology,* P. Brown (ed.), pp. 190–220. Belmont: Wadsworth.

Roberts, H. (1981) Women and their doctors: power and powerlessness in the research process. In *Doing Feminist Research,* H. Roberts (ed.), pp. 7–29. London: Routledge and Kegan Paul.

Robertson, A. (1982) The pain of labor: a time of growth. *New Parent,* **2,** 9–12.

Rodell, S. (1985) The late baby boom. *The National Times,* April 12, 9–10.

Romalis, S. (1981) *Childbirth: Alternatives to Medical Control.* Austin: University of Texas Press.

Rose, H. (1986) Women's work, women's knowledge. In *What is Feminism?,* J. Mitchell and A. Oakley (eds), pp. 161–183. New York: Pantheon.

Rose, M. A. (1991) *The Post-modern and the Post-industrial.* Cambridge: Cambridge University Press.

Rosengren, W. R. (1962) Social sources of pregnancy as illness or normality. *Social Forces,* **9,** 260–267.

Rothman, B. K. (1988) The decision to have or not to have amniocentesis for prenatal diagnosis. In *Childbirth in America. Anthropological Perspectives,* K. L. Michaelson (ed.), pp. 90–102. South Hadley, Mass.: Bergin and Garvey.

Rothman, B. K. (1989) *Recreating Motherhood: Ideology and technology in a Patriarchal Society.* New York: W.W.Norton.

Rowland, R. (1988) *Woman Herself.* Melbourne: Oxford University Press.

Rowland, R. (1990) *Living Laboratories: Women and Reproductive Technology.* Bloomington: Indiana University Press.

Rowland, R. (1991) Motherhood and foetal personhood: the challenge of women's reproductive control from reproductive technology. Paper presented at the Australian Sociological Association Conference, Murdoch University, Perth.

Ruddick, S. (1980) Maternal Thinking. *Feminist Studies,* **6,** (2), 342–423.

Ruddick, S. (1989) *Maternal Thinking: Towards a Politics of Peace.* Boston: Beacon Press.

Russell, G. (1983) *The Changing Role of Fathers.* St. Lucia: University of Queensland Press.

Rybczynski, W. (1986) *Home. A Short History of an Idea.* New York: Penguin.

Salleh, K. (1981) Of Portnoy's complaint and feminist problematics: A reconciliation with critical theory. *Australian and New Zealand Journal of Sociology,* **17,** (1), 4–13.

Schloten, C. M. (1977) On the importance of the obstetrick art: changing customs of childbirth in America, 1760 to 1825. *William and Mary Quarterly,* **34** (3rd ser.), 426–445.

Scutt, J. A. (ed.) (1988) *The Baby Machine: Commercialisation of Motherhood.* Carlton, Vic: McCulloch.

Selitz, C., Jahoda, M., Deutsch, M. and Cook, S. W. (1962) *Research Methods in Social Relations.* New York: Holt, Rinehart and Winston.

Shorter, E. (1984) *A History of Women's Bodies.* Harmondsworth: Penguin.

Silverman, D. (1985) *Qualitative Methodology and Sociology.* Aldershot: Gower.

Simpson, L. (1988) The birth and death of Kiah Jeanes. *Good Weekend,* October 8, 12–20.

Sinclair, W. G. (1980) *The Process of Economic Development in Australia.* Melbourne: Longman Cheshire.

Smith, D. E. (1988 [1987]) *The Everyday World as Problematic: A Feminist Sociology.* Oxford: Open University Press/Milton Keyes.

Social Impacts (1987) Minutes of the Post Natal Depression Workshop, Sydney.

Sontag, S. (1978) *Illness as Metaphor.* New York: Vintage.

Soper, K. (1990) *Troubled Pleasures.* London: Verso.

Spensky, M. (1992) Producers of legitimacy: homes for unmarried mothers in the 1950s. In *Regulating Womanhood. Historical Essays on Marriage, Motherhood and Sexuality,* C. Smart (ed.), pp. 100–118. London and New York: Routledge.

Stanley, L. and Wise, S. (1979) Feminist research, feminist consciousness and experience of sexism. *Women's Studies International Quarterly,* **2,** (3), 359–374.

Stanworth, M. (ed.) (1987) *Reproductive Technologies. Gender, Motherhood and Medicine.* Minneapolis: University of Minnesota Press.

Stern, G. and Kruckman, L. (1987) Multi-disciplinary perspectives on postpartum depression: an anthropological critique. *Social Science and Medicine,* **17,** (15), 1027–1041.

Strauss, A. and Corbin, J. (1990) *Basics of Qualitative Research. Grounded Theory, Procedures and Techniques.* Newbury Park: Sage.

Tanzer, D. with Blocj, J. L. (1976) *Why Natural Childbirth? A Psychologists's Report on the Benefits to Mothers, Fathers and Babies.* New York: Schocken Books.

Taylor, R. (1982) The birth of Sky. *Homebirth Access Sydney Newsletter,* **1,** 6–7.

Terry, D. J. (1991) Predictors of subjective stress in a sample of new parents. *Australian Journal of Psychology,* **43,** (1), 29–36.

Tew, A. (1986) Do obstetric intranatal interventions make birth safe? *British Journal of Obstetrics and Gynaecology,* **93,** (7), 659–674.

Thiele, B. (1986) Vanishing acts in social and political thought: Tricks of the trade. In *Feminist Challenges: Social and Political Theory,* C. Pateman and E. Gross (eds), pp. 30–43. Sydney: Allen and Unwin.

Thomas, D. B. (1986) Obstetric intervention and its effect on the baby. Paper presented at a Conference on Birth: A Normal Process? Hazards of Medical Intervention, Centre for Continuing Education, Australian National University, Canberra.

Thomas, W. I. and Znaniecki, F. (1918) *The Polish Peasant in Europe and America.* Chicago: University of Chicago Press.

Tilly, C. (1985) Models and realities of popular collective action. *Social Research*, **52**, (4), 717–747.

Toliver, S. D. (1986) 20/20 vision: A perspective on women's changing roles and the structure of American families, past and future. *Frontiers*, **9**, (1), 27–31.

Touraine, A. (1984) The waning sociological image of social life. In *The Global Crisis*, E. A. Tiriyakin (ed.), pp. 33–44. Leiden: E. J. Brill.

Turner, V. and Turner, E. (1978) *Image and Pilgrimage in Christian Cultures*. New York: Columbia University Press.

van Gennep, A. (1960) *Rites of Passage*. London: Routledge and Kegan Paul.

van Vucht Tijssen, L. (1990) Women between modernity and post-modernity. In *Theories of Modernity and Postmodernity*, B. S. Turner (ed.), pp. 147–163. London: Sage.

Walker, R. (1985) An introduction to qualitative research. In *Applied Qualitative Research*, R. Walker (ed.), pp. 3–26. Aldershot: Gower.

Wearing, B. (1984) *The Ideology of Motherhood*. Sydney: George Allen and Unwin.

Weber, M. (1958) *The Protestant Ethic and the Spirit of Capitalism*. New York: Charles Scribner & Sons.

Weedon, C. (1987) *Feminist Practice and Post-Structuralist Theory*. Oxford: Blackwell.

Welburn, V. (1980) *Postnatal Depression*. Glasgow: Fontana.

Wiles, J. (1985) The stormy sequel to Ebony's 'gentle' waterbirth. *New Idea*, 3 August, 16–17.

Williams, N. (1975) *Chronology of the Modern World*. Harmondsworth: Penguin.

Woliver, L. R. (1991) The influence of technology on the politics of motherhood. An overview of the United States. *Women's Studies International Forum*, **14**, (5), 479–490.

Women's Health Issues (1991) *Special Issue on Surrogacy*, **1**, 3.

Wright, E. (1974) *The New Childbirth*. London: Tandem.

Zijderveld, A. C. (1974) *The Abstract Society*. Harmondsworth: Penguin.

Znaniecki, F. (1934) *The Method of Sociology*. New York: Rinehart.

INDEX